STOP
THE CHURCH'S
REVOLVING DOOR

STOP
THE CHURCH'S
REVOLVING DOOR

BUILDING RELATIONSHIPS WITH CHURCH MEMBERS

DR. RICHARD M. WRIGHT

WestBow
PRESS
A DIVISION OF THOMAS NELSON

WestBow Press books may be ordered through booksellers or by contacting:

WestBow Press
A Division of Thomas Nelson
1663 Liberty Drive
Bloomington, IN 47403
www.westbowpress.com
1-(866) 928-1240

Because of the dynamic nature of the Internet, any web addresses or links contained in this book may have changed since publication and may no longer be valid. The views expressed in this work are solely those of the author and do not necessarily reflect the views of the publisher, and the publisher hereby disclaims any responsibility for them.

Any people depicted in stock imagery provided by Thinkstock are models, and such images are being used for illustrative purposes only.

Certain stock imagery © Thinkstock.

ISBN: 978-1-4497-3451-0 (sc)
ISBN: 978-1-4497-3452-7 (hc)
ISBN: 978-1-4497-3450-3 (e)

Library of Congress Control Number: 2011963013

Printed in the United States of America

WestBow Press rev. date: 12/23/2011

Dedication

To my wife and daughter, who endured several years
of research and writing for this book and still love me
because of God's love that dwells within them.

Contents

Preface

This project is several years in the making. It began as an implementation of a new ministry in a church. It continued in another church with several improvements. Now, it has evolved into a book for use in your church or ministry.

I disclose later why building relationships within the church is important to me. Suffice it to say at this point, the Christian church is all about building, nurturing, and maintaining relationships with God and other church members.

Thanks to Reverend Mark Hunnicutt of Mud Creek Baptist Church in Hendersonville, North Carolina. His C.A.R.E. Ministry served as an impetus for this relationship building ministry.

A hearty thank-you to the Lakeland United Methodist Church for being brave enough to implement and improve this new ministry. This book would not be possible without your help.

Kathy Miller was a tremendous help in editing the manuscript. Her tireless efforts taught me more about grammar and composition than what I recalled from high school and college.

I pray that you enjoy this book. God blessed me tremendously while working on it. I hope that you are blessed by the presence of the Holy Spirit as you read about this ministry. I especially pray for God's guidance when you implement this ministry. It will be worthwhile!

May the love, grace, and mercy of God the Father; the salvation that comes only through Jesus Christ the Son; and the most awesome power of the Holy Spirit go with you now and forevermore. Amen!

Chapter 1

The Problem

Church members cease active church participation for many reasons. This can be viewed as an epidemic within mainline denominations, including the United Methodist Church (UMC) where I have pastored for 14 years. Some have described the local church as having a revolving door, with newcomers joining even as disgruntled members leave. First-time and regular visitors also use this revolving door when the church's members do not reach out to them in an effort to begin the relationship-building process.

When church members cease active participation, there is a severing of relationships between them and the church. In most churches, the clergy and laypeople allow these relationships to remain severed. During the research that resulted in this book, I found that most churches do little or nothing to reach out to let absent members know they are missed. When the member is absent for several weeks, the relationship has been severed and church members have no idea how to repair it. They don't know what to say to the now-inactive church member. Some may be afraid that they are the reason someone left the church, and that if they go and talk with the inactive church member, they may exacerbate the situation in such a way that the inactive person will never return to active church participation.

This book addresses two key questions regarding church participation:

- How can the local church begin to repair severed relationships?
- What tactics can help the church decrease the number of long-term inactive members who use that revolving door?

I have discovered that most churches, regardless of denominational affiliation, do not have a ministry or structure to help active members reach out to inactive members in order to maintain and/or reestablish relationships. A few years ago as the senior pastor of Lakeland United Methodist Church (LUMC), I realized that we failed to stay relationally connected to our inactive members. We were allowing short-term inactive members to become long-term inactive members. Our lack of action— due at least in part to the lack of a structured ministry addressing the problem—caused the revolving door to spin even more quickly. Something had to be done. The C.A.R.E. (Christians Actively Reaching Everyone) ministry developed by Mark Hunnicutt was used in a church I had served previously. This provided a starting point. I believed that this ministry could serve LUMC well in developing a ministry targeting inactive members.

This book describes our journey toward designing and implementing a caring ministry to reach out to long-term inactive members. We used the ministry techniques to interdict members early on, with a goal of preventing long-term church absenteeism. Our hope was that the number of inactive members would decrease and our church would become healthier with the interactive presence of more church members.

Our church's revolving door slowed dramatically thanks to this caring ministry. While this book focuses on working with inactive members, I will discuss the expansion of this ministry to visitors and active church members (which Mark Hunnicutt suggests in his ministry manual) near the conclusion.

My pastoral perspective is inherently United Methodist, since I am an ordained elder within the UMC. However, this ministry approach can be implemented in any church of any size with few modifications to its structure. This ministry is not designed to be a *cookie cutter ministry* where you strictly implement only what you find here. It should be modified to exist alongside your church's existing ministries. It is neither a replacement nor a substitute ministry to what you and your church are already doing. Rather, it is offered to enhance your ability to slow your church's revolving door.

Significance of the Problem

A caring ministry for relationship building is very important to me as a way to help inactive members uphold the membership vow and return to active church participation. When people join the UMC, they vow to be loyal to Jesus Christ through the UMC by upholding it "with their presence, prayers, gifts, service, and witness" (UMC *Discipline*, 143). When I joined the UMC in the early 1980s, my pastor told me that Jesus Christ calls all Christians to be in fellowship with each other as a way to support each other's spiritual journey. Hebrews 10:25 reminds us not to forsake assembling together, which enables us to be in a supportive fellowship. He explained that fulfillment of the membership vow helps United Methodists to remain relationally connected to God, the universal Church, the UMC, and to the other members within our church.

As I grew in my faith, I realized relationships helped me keep my membership vow. I also noticed how other church members were fulfilling their membership vow. I saw the vow's fulfillment through the lens of church participation. Some upheld their vows in an exemplary manner through a high level of church participation. The level of church participation seemed to correlate with the quality of the personal relationships church members had with one another. Those who had a high level of participation had a large number of relationships with other church members. They also had personal relationships with others outside the faith community, but their church relationships helped them to fulfill their membership vow.

I did not fully understand the effect of upholding the membership vow until I became a lay leader in a small congregation. The pastor encouraged all members to spread Christ's gospel by serving in the church's ministries, but only a small number of them were active. The old adage that I have heard a number of times is called the 80-20 Rule: 80 percent of church work is done by 20 percent of the church members. My personal church participation and observations within several churches of several denominations would change that rule to the 95-10 Rule: 95 percent of church work is accomplished by 10 percent of the church members.

When I became a UMC pastor, I realized that my home church was not the only church with this problem. After several years serving as a pastor in small to medium to large churches, I wondered if upholding the membership vow could be encouraged by establishing, maintaining, and enhancing the relationships among church members.

As senior pastor of LUMC, I realized that our church was not encouraging inactive members to return to active church life. Once a church member became inactive, the church's lack of action essentially severed the relationship with that member. The only contact the church had with inactive members was through the mailing of weekly church bulletins.

My pastoral instinct urged me to stop allowing the severing of these relationships and to find a way to begin rebuilding them. As a church, we had to develop the means to *catch* people who were not actively participating in the life of the church before they walked through the church's revolving door for the last time.

With this burning issue churning inside of me, I turned to church growth materials to see if they could help with ministry development. I went to one of the best-selling church growth books, *The Purpose Driven Church* by Rick Warren, the senior pastor of Saddleback Church. Warren has many great things to say about church growth being accomplished "primarily through relationships" (Warren, 173). He admits that "the church is not called to do one thing; it is called to do many things" (Warren, 128). He even uses the apostle Paul's analogy, where the body is a "system of interworking parts and organs" (Warren, 128). However, I disagree with Warren on a fundamental level when it comes to reaching out to inactive members.

Warren's stance is that the church should not do anything with inactive members. In the chapter titled "Organizing Around Your Purposes," he implies that churches should not worry about inactive members and advocates removing them from the membership roll by "redefining the meaning of membership" (Warren, 133). I view this as pushing inactive members completely out of the church and implying that they are no longer wanted or needed.

Warren believes that a church should focus on bringing new members into the church and not "waste time" reaching out to the inactive members. He explains why his church does not pursue inactive members in the chapter titled "Knowing Whom You Can Best Reach." To his way of thinking, growing churches focus on reaching receptive people, whereas "non-growing churches focus on re-enlisting inactive people" (Warren, 183). He further states that it "takes about five times more energy to reactivate a disgruntled or carnal member than it does to win a receptive believer" (Warren, 183).

While I believe that several of Pastor Warren's thoughts are right on the mark (especially those concerning visioning and reaching out into the community to share the good news of Christ with unbelievers), I believe that churches should also reach *into* their congregations to re-evangelize those members whose Holy Spirit-driven fire has waned. The body of Christ—also known as the church—must not push inactive members to the side.

In the next chapter, I provide some scriptural perspectives regarding my theological position when it comes to how the local church is called to reach out to *inactives*. In *The Purpose Driven Church,* Pastor Warren alludes to the apostle Paul's passage on the body of Christ, but I will further expand on that passage in regards to why we cannot allow relationships with members to be deleted from our memory in favor of pursuing new Christians.

Based on Scripture, I surmise that both our church and our community will benefit from the participation and service of inactive people who return to active church participation. More importantly, all of us can benefit on a personal level from reestablished relationships.

Significance of the Problem to LUMC

I will be using LUMC as a model for local churches. No matter what size your church is, your church may have the same issue within its membership. Most churches have a large number of inactive members on their membership rolls, especially well-established churches or churches whose polity will not allow instant removal for inactivity.

LUMC is located in the South Georgia Annual Conference of the UMC. At the end of 2007, LUMC reported 386 members with an average Sunday morning worship attendance of 117. Only 30 percent of church members attended church on a regular basis! This statistic was close to what I had been told in seminary and what I had experienced as a lay leader within several churches. Having been the pastor-in-charge of several UM churches, I found that this was the rule instead of the exception. I discovered through many discussions with other pastors and lay leaders that well-established churches within my annual conference experienced this same problem.

Our Sunday School saw eighty-one people on the rolls with an average weekly attendance of forty-nine. Only 13 percent of church members attended Sunday School! Being a medium-size church of more than three hundred members, Sunday School was the primary weekly Christian education endeavor because more people attended Sunday School than the midweek Bible studies.

What can LUMC do to increase the participation of all of its members? How can LUMC stop this revolving door where people come in and seem to be going right back out weeks, months, or years after beginning their relationship within the church as a member?

These statistics indicated the need for a caring ministry that would empower active members to become more involved in improving the church's health through reaching out to rebuild relationships with inactive members. The church has ministries that attract visitors and assist them in becoming mature Christians to the point of joining the church's membership. However, there is no caring ministry that focused on maintaining strong relationships that aid in active church participation. Thus, the means to stop the church's revolving door!

As the new pastor, I found LUMC to be like other churches where I had been a member or pastor. LUMC was weak in lay empowerment. The lay leaders expressed concerns about lay empowerment during my initial meetings with them. The lay leadership assisted me in implementing several endeavors focusing on lay empowerment. The first effort was training of the lay leadership on local church leader responsibilities. This training resulted in increased confidence by the lay leaders in their leadership abilities and on exercising their leadership responsibilities. It also helped in the various ministry committees developing, implementing, and executing ministries that addressed several issues within our church and community.

The second venture guided the lay leadership to focus on its church health. During the lay empowerment phase, the lay leaders saw that if they were to fulfill God's call for their church, then they would have to improve their church's health. The result of this venture was the identification of strong and weak areas in which to develop the means to address health issues. This identification equipped the church lay leadership to move into the last endeavor. The last endeavor was the church's efforts to implement a Church Health Action Plan. This plan was the result of many months of work.

The lay leaders believed that improvement of the church's health was necessary. They addressed their church health through Natural Church Development (NCD). NCD is a process developed by Christian Schwarz and the Institute for NCD. This process focuses on the improvement on the church's lowest-rated quality characteristic. The church discovered this weak area through a scientific survey completed by active church members. Survey results revealed that "needs-oriented evangelism" was LUMC's lowest-rated characteristic.

The congregation and its Church Health Team worked together to develop a Church Health Action Plan with three ministry priorities. One of the priorities called for a visitation ministry with inactive members. The ministry's goal is to help inactive members return to active church participation.

The lay leadership recognized that personal relationships were the primary reason most of them came to LUMC. They believed that reestablished relationships could encourage inactive members to return to active church participation. They also thought that enhancing relationships with existing members and church visitors could result in increases in ministry and worship attendance.

During the work on the Church Health Action Plan, one returned inactive member stated, "The church did not care for me when I dropped out from church." When asked why he felt this way, he stated, "No one called or visited me until the pastor visited after his arrival which was several years after I stopped coming to church." This may be the impression of many inactive members, but it is not the attitude of the active church members. The congregation expressed its concern for all church members but lacked the means and vision to demonstrate this care to inactive members. The Church Health Action Plan was the church's way to provide a viable solution to this issue.

Lay personal contacts could be helpful in reconnecting with inactive members and enhancing relationships with visitors. My personal experience shows that laypeople expect a pastor to visit because pastors are paid to do so. In my own denomination, our church polity tasks clergy to "visit in the homes of the church and the community" (UMC *Discipline*, 251) and the local church to help "its members uphold their membership vows" (UMC *Discipline*, 149). However, LUMC did not have a visitation ministry conducted by lay people. The congregation identified this as a significant ministry weakness.

The LUMC membership statistics are deceiving. We discovered that there was no contact information for 121 members. This indicates weak relationship building when one-third of the members have no contact information. Of the 265 left, one hundred live out of town. Only 117 of the remaining 165 members actively participate through church worship attendance. Forty-eight people are local, inactive members.

How depressing are these numbers? LUMC had 69 percent of its membership not attending church on a regular basis for a variety of reasons. Many of these reasons we did not know about.

A more depressing thought is that almost one-third of the local members are inactive. This shows that personal relationships among our church members are weak. It was past time for our congregation to work on its relationship building. Our congregation was willing to work on its weakness through the implementation of a caring ministry.

Are these statistics similar to what you are experiencing in your church? Yes! Then continue to read on about how this problem is significant to a mainline denomination.

Significance of the Problem to the UMC at Large

I have been a pastor in several UMC churches in South Georgia. All failed to stay relationally connected to inactive members. None of these churches, which were small to large churches, had a structured ministry to nurture the personal relationships that had been established. There was no structure within the churches to help reconnect to those who walked out the revolving door. If this problem exists in my church, then what would this issue look like across the UMC in the United States?

In 2000, the UMC reported that there were 8,249,579 lay church members in the United States. It also reported that 41.8 percent of these members attended worship on an average. This means that the statistics are much better than LUMC, but this still means that 3.5 million people have severed relationships with their church!

How much more relevant and productive could the UMC be if we could have 3.5 million members become active again in their local churches? How exciting would church be to have about 1.75 million people attending Sunday School on a regular basis?

Since 1970, the UMC in the United States has been in a steady decline. In 1970, the American UMC boasted 10,671,774 lay members. By 2000, there was a decline of more than 2 million members or a 22 percent slide. These numbers should serve as a call to action for the UMC!

It is time for us to stop the revolving door that is resulting in our church's decline. This decline is having a major effect on the UMC's ability to make and nurture disciples for Christ and in sharing the good news of Christ in the world.

The Methodist heritage began when John Wesley established societies where laypeople had personal relationships with other society members. These relationships encouraged church members to grow spiritually and exhibit this growth in holy living. These societies were created "to nurture a deeper love of God, which members would manifest in the practice of Christian love" (Frank, 46).

Personal relationships appeared to help the Methodist Societies accomplish this nurturing, which will be explored later. Today, there are many competing interests with local church activities. With these competing secular interests, church members do not exercise the same level of accountability as the Wesleyan societies. However, today's church lay and clergy leadership must develop ministries that help nurture personal relationships that enhance faith in God and work toward building up of God's kingdom. This building up is not just in numerical increases in the membership roll but in actually active church participation.

I have already shown you that a large percentage of the church's membership is inactive. If local UM churches could implement a ministry that helps reconnect to inactive members, then the UMC might become stronger with more active church members. Although bringing unchurched people into the UMC remains a top priority, we must not forget the inactive members who also need spiritual growth. If we could use this same new ministry to reaching out to our inactive members, then we may see a rise in worship attendance. This rise in worship attendance could evolve into greater participation in the church's Christian education endeavors.

Abraham Maslow proposed a theory called the hierarchy of needs in his 1943 paper titled "A Theory of Human Motivation." This theory proposes five levels of human needs. In order of priority, they are physiological, safety, belonging, esteem, and self-actualization. The need to belong achieves an acceptable comfort level when people develop personal relationships with family members and others.

> After physiological and safety needs are fulfilled, the third layer of human needs is social. This psychological aspect of Maslow's hierarchy involves emotionally-based relationships in general, such as friendship, intimacy, and having a supportive family. Humans need to feel a sense of belonging and acceptance, whether it comes from a large social group (clubs, office culture, religious groups, professional organizations, sports teams, or gangs) or small social connections (family members, intimate partners, mentors, close colleagues, or confidants). They need to love and be loved (sexually and non-sexually) by others. In the absence of these elements, many people become susceptible to loneliness, anxiety, and clinical depression.

This social need can be partially met when the local church's ministries help people develop personal relationships whereby the individual feels nurtured and cared for. The church's ministries can help the congregation express its concern for fellow members. A caring ministry can help active and inactive members reconnect with each other whereby inactive members are invited to return to active church participation with a renewed sense of belonging.

The significance of this issue to the UMC is that all church members need to be actively connected to the church. The church's ministries need to facilitate the building of authentic personal relationships so that fewer church members become inactive through the revolving door. Establishing new churches can help increase the number of people attending and/or joining the UMC, but eventually these new churches will face the same issues as the well-established churches detailed earlier.

In order to stop the revolving door, we must do something radical! Radicalism is seen in evangelizing within our own congregations by working with our inactive church members. This caring ministry would be implemented so God is glorified with more disciples of Christ serving through active participation within the body of Christ and not for the glory of your church or denomination.

Nature and Purpose of the Ministry

At this point, I think that it would be helpful for you to have an understanding of this new ministry that I am proposing. Looking at what occurred at my church while we implemented this ministry can help you implement it at your church. My focus will be discussing the work with inactive members. We did not expand this caring ministry until after our evaluation phase, which is detailed in a later chapter.

We will look at how effectively this caring ministry was in rebuilding authentic personal relationships with inactive members. This book is written for pastors and congregations who desire to rebuild relationships with inactive members. It is also for those pastors and congregations who want to decrease or eliminate the opportunity for short-term inactive members to become long-term inactives. This is for those who want to stop the fast-moving revolving-church membership door!

Our objective is to build authentic personal relationships with inactive members through a caring ministry. The intent of this ministry is not to coerce inactives back to worship attendance but to take steps toward active church participation. The hope is that these steps will ultimately lead inactive members and visitors toward "active fellowship within the church" (Frank, 163).

This Is My Community

For you to understand the context in which we implemented this ministry, I need to provide you with details about our community and church. Your community and church will be different because there is only one Lakeland, Georgia, and only one LUMC. Therefore you will need to take an objective look at your context so that you can modify this caring ministry to work effectively in your church and community.

Lakeland, Georgia, is the seat of Lanier County. It is located twenty miles northeast of the Valdosta metropolitan area. Lakeland's history is captured in murals that are painted on the original city buildings. The older members of the community have a passion to remember the past days. This passion finds its way into the church through our older church members, particularly those members who were born and raised in Lakeland.

According to the latest demographics, the population of Lanier County is 5,098. The population's genders are evenly divided. The ethnic makeup is white (57.2 percent), black (39.3 percent), Hispanic (1.2 percent), and three other races (2.3 percent). The median household income is $22,346, which is almost $20,000 under the national average. Farming and retail trade dominate the job market. The job market is directly connected to Lanier County's low educational level where over 36 percent of adults do not possess a high school diploma. This level is much lower than state and national averages.

Farming influences 90 percent of the church's families. This influence periodically affects the church during sowing and harvest times with low worship attendance and financial giving. The church is dependent on the success of the crops to fund the church's ministries.

There are sixty-eight Christian churches in Lanier County. Seventeen are within the Lakeland city limits. This overabundance of churches challenges LUMC to sustain the participation of its church members because of transfers to other churches.

These demographic factors may explain why some church members have become inactive. They may also provide us with a picture of why visitors do not return. However, these factors did not adversely affect the implementation of a caring ministry but provided us with encouragement to move forward unafraid.

This Is My Church

LUMC is the oldest church in Lakeland. It was established as part of a multi-church charge in 1856. In the 1940s, the church became a station church with its own pastor. The church was built on its present location in 1948. The church added additional Sunday School rooms and a fellowship hall in 1984. The campus expanded in 2007 with the purchase of two buildings that house our youth and scouting ministries. The lay leadership committed to expansion of the church campus while declining in church membership. This expansion may increase worship attendance and financial giving.

The church relies on history to guide its future decisions. The passion for historical things is evident at LUMC with several members related to the city's founding families. These members recall that church membership required little effort. "Everyone is a church member somewhere in town," is often quoted. This historical perspective may affect the number of people volunteering for the caring ministry because they do not see the need for this kind of ministry. It is also possible that people do not volunteer for this ministry because they did not have this ministry in the past.

The LUMC congregation does not mirror the county's demographics. The average LUMC worshipper is a well-educated female in her late fifties. Several professional people and wealthy families are active at LUMC. The education level of the lay leadership helps in effective planning of ministries. They have demonstrated this in the recent implementation of several ministries. The material wealth of the congregation enables them to fund the ministries they deem necessary.

I discovered local citizens view LUMC as "the rich white church." I attribute this perception to two factors. First, it is rare for other races to attend LUMC. Second, many prominent business and community leaders attend LUMC. Active church members do not accept this community perspective. They see themselves as good Christians serving God in nurturing ways. The "rich white church" moniker creates a dilemma for a caring ministry because this stigma may be a reason for church inactivity and could hamper relationship building.

Active members view their collective personality as caring and loving. A pastoral visit revealed this feeling. A member was absent because of illness. She said people visited and called during her absence. This is one example that shows active members who exhibit a caring attitude toward other active members. Several inactive members expressed experiences of uncaring attitudes by active members. These contrasting perspectives led the lay leaders to guide the church toward a caring ministry.

The desire to improve their church health may help in recruiting volunteers. The caring ministry would give active members the venue to demonstrate their love and care for all members. However, members believing that they care enough through existing ministries could hamper the project.

LUMC is the only UM church within the city limits. The pastors of the other city churches have been in place for many years. Based on discussions with the local ministerial association, no churches in Lanier County have a caring ministry for inactive members. This could affect the project in two ways. The negative aspect is that members will not implement the ministry because it has not been tried in Lakeland. The positive aspect is that other churches may implement this ministry if LUMC's endeavor proves successful.

When compared to these other churches, LUMC is what Carl Dudley calls the pillar church. Dudley is the Professor of Church and Community at Union Theological Seminary. "The pillar church is anchored in its community, a place for which it feels a distinct responsibility. The architecture often reflects this self-image—strong pillars that lift the roof physically and the community spiritually. Like the building, the members are pillars of the community, good citizens individually and corporately. Resources of heritage, leadership, facilities, and finances are used to strengthen the whole community" (Dudley, 4).

The church takes pride in its special events, which include homecoming, Christmas, and Vacation Bible School. LUMC is a conservative United Methodist church located in a politically and religiously conservative county seat. This theological stance affects the ministries of the congregation. Church members implementing new ministries must target people with the same conservative perspectives. If a ministry resembles this stance, then there is a greater possibility of its acceptance among the congregation. This stance is not expected to affect the caring ministry because the inactive members typically have the same theological and political viewpoints.

The members' work ethic is tremendous, which is exemplified with the maintenance on our church buildings. Church members perform most of the maintenance work themselves. The members also fund renovation projects without incurring any debt. This shows that church members can and will work toward goals they deem worthy. Since the congregation helped to establish the Church Health Action Plan priorities, this may increase the likelihood of a successful volunteer recruitment campaign.

Church members describe the church's dynamics as "family." Many families are related to each other by birth or marriage. These relationships form a community power structure. The families with ties to the pioneers of Lakeland exercise more influence in the community and church decision-making processes. With the support of these influential people, the church accomplishes special community events with few distractions. For the ministry to be implemented, these influential people will need to give their approval. Some of these people helped craft the Church Health Action Plan, which should eliminate this particular obstacle.

The church sees itself as an open system. This means it gives outsiders the opportunity to become church members and/or participate in the church's ministries. However, these outsiders do not become insiders until they have been in the church for many years. There is the possibility that new people cannot become insiders if they are radically different from the church's demographics, political leanings, or theological perspectives. The caring ministry's efforts in rebuilding relationships could be hampered if the inactive members are viewed as outsiders. Re-established relationships can be severely disabled if other active members treat them as outsiders upon their return.

The LUMC family system is not as open as the active members believe. They have not maintained contact with the inactive members or those who moved away. The lack of contact may cause inactive members to move farther away from the church. In family systems language, under-functioning is occurring. The congregation under-functions in reaching out while inactive members under-function by withdrawing. A caring ministry would enable the church to move toward inactive members. The ministry would enable inactive members to reconnect to the body of Christ at LUMC. The hope is that they will become comfortable enough to rejoin the life of the church as active members.

There are four congregational anxiety triggers at LUMC: pastoral transitions, lay leadership style, pastoral leadership style, and long-term commitments. The first anxiety is caused by the appointed pastors' short tenures. Pastoral transitions occur every three to four years. This periodic turnover results in a seemingly constant state of pastoral transition. In this church during my transition, few ministries continued. This trigger points out the need for lay leadership empowerment. Empowerment could result in a more dominant role for the laity in ministry decision making. The caring ministry is a result of this lay empowerment. However this caring ministry can be in jeopardy when the next pastoral transition occurs. A greater chance of survival is possible if the lay leadership continues to exercise shared leadership roles.

Pastoral transition anxiety leads to the second concern of lay leadership style. With a rare exception, the lay leadership is overly dependent on the pastor. In the absence of pastoral guidance, the lay leadership allows a few people to influence the church's ministry direction. Some lay leaders complain about this situation but are reluctant to take any actions to correct it. This anxiety can hamper the caring ministry implementation through the lay leaders' support of the ministry. Ministry implementation needs the support of the church's influential members in order to have any possibility of success.

The third trigger is pastoral leadership style. Members claim that LUMC's success is traditionally dependent on the pastor. This is not acceptable because of periodic pastoral changes due to the UMC's clergy appointment system. There is a need to return to the Methodist heritage of lay leadership whereby the lay leadership has shared leadership roles with the pastor. This would allow the pastor to assume a significant but not dominant leadership role within the ministry decision-making process. Over the last two years, the congregation has made progress toward these shared leadership roles and less dependence on the pastor. These roles encouraged lay leaders to develop the Church Health Action Plan that led to this project. However, some leaders still want the pastor to dictate the ministries.

The last anxiety trigger is long-term commitments. Church members resist long-term commitments that require weekly attendance. This observation is based on low attendance at our Wednesday night Bible studies, youth and children Bible studies, and missions work. This observation was confirmed by our lay leadership's work on the Church Health Action Plan. Their explanation is the heavy participation of members in secular associations. When discussing a visitation ministry, I posed a question: "If we were to start a visitation ministry, what day of the week would be best?" The lay leaders talked about the community's political, fraternal, civic, and recreational groups. They determined the best time would be the evening and the best day would be Tuesday night. This was based on fewer secular events in the community to compete with the new ministry. They also indicated that each night should last no more than two hours. The scheduling may influence the size of the volunteer pool and the number of visits conducted each week.

The congregation emphasizes the need to create relationships with all church members and visitors. Through these relationships, we can encourage each other to be and become faithful members of the body of Christ. As LUMC implements this caring ministry, the active members will be returning to their Methodist heritage of lay involvement and participation. Their involvement in the caring ministry may connect them with the scriptural and theological insights found in the next chapters.

Chapter 2

Scriptural Insights

The previous chapter portrays LUMC as a church divided along social-class lines. My pastoral experience shows that division and conflict within the church is common and continuous. This contradicts the belief of many people that the church is harmonious and united. Church members struggle with living up to the lifestyle standards expressed in Scripture. LUMC and its members, and probably your church, face this same struggle. We first come to Scripture to discern guidance to overcome present cultural divisions within the church in an effort to build positive personal relationships.

Conflict sources are unique to each church, but the result is the same: people become alienated about the church. Some people become so alienated that they abandon the church to attend another church or stop attending church altogether. Herb Miller, who is an internationally recognized authority on congregational health and effectiveness with sixteen books, identified twenty reasons that cause people to walk out of the church's revolving door (Miller, 3).

1. Conflict with the pastor;
2. Conflict with another church member;
3. Feeling unaccepted by other church members;
4. Assimilation failures (not fit into the church's environment);
5. Change in pastors;
6. Insufficient friendship formation;
7. Feeling neglected during or after a personal tragedy;
8. The overworked, burned-out syndrome (overly involved in church ministries);
9. Too little change in the church;

10. Conflict with a family member;
11. Various forms of life crisis;
12. Various forms of life change;
13. Moral problem;
14. Failing Band-Aid syndrome (life's problems were not solved by church involvement);
15. Cultural differences;
16. Lack of shared theological values;
17. Lifestyle incompatibility;
18. Control failure (control not being obtained or control being overly exerted upon);
19. Fear of any conflict; and
20. Angry unwillingness to rebuild broken relationships.

No matter what the cause of the person walking out the revolving door, the alienation and absence of these people who were involved in the church cause the church to be less effective in ministry. There is scriptural evidence that encourages us to seek ways to reach out to those who have been involved in the church. This evidence shows that conflict and the revolving door have been around since the advent of the Christian church.

Apostle Paul's letters seem to indicate that the early church constantly struggled with divisions. In 1 Corinthians, Paul encountered many different sources of church division. His writings provide recommendations through a visible comparison on how the church can overcome these divisions through unity and relationships.

Is the context of ancient Corinth similar to LUMC or your church? To answer this question, we will briefly discuss the city of Corinth, the Christian church establishment, and the writing of 1 Corinthians. This brief study of 1 Corinthians will provide us with an understanding of Paul's view of the church as a united body where members relate to each other and help the church's ministries to be more effective.

The City of Corinth

Corinth was established as the capital of the Roman province of Achaia. With its establishment on a major trade route, Corinth became a major urban center with commercial and financial importance. The commercial importance of the city came from its location on the Isthmus of Corinth. This location provided for a short trade route across Greece, which spared trade ships from sailing around the southern tip of Greece. Commercial trade resulted in Corinth becoming a financial center. The city's mercantile and monetary importance contributed to Corinth becoming a culturally diverse city.

This diversity had effects on the citizens' roles. In his commentary on 1 Corinthians, Keener noted, "Roles were determined by social status in antiquity, and those with wealth and power preferred religious, philosophical and political ideologies that supported their base of power." Status was demonstrated through the common Greco-Roman practice of the wealthy citizens receiving "higher quality and quantity of food, and the poor members going without" (Coutsoumpos 1). The Corinthian citizenship was divided along material wealth lines into wealthy and poor social groups.

Polytheism increased with the city's population diversity. The trading culture increased the presence of other religious beliefs, including paganism. The amount of religious edifices in Corinth were "symbolic of the domination" of pagan polytheism (Buttrick, 3). Polytheism, when combined with its use for social status, further divided the Corinthian population.

Amid the pagan polytheism, the Jewish monotheistic worship was viewed as countercultural. Jews in the Roman Empire lived in relative harmony. However, their religious practices were so different from the majority of the Corinthian citizens that the Jewish people were unpopular. Low acceptance by most of the Corinthian society caused the Jewish community to separate itself from the Gentiles in social and religious areas. This separation could limit the potential of Jewish merchants in Corinth. Therefore the Jewish citizens could not enter into the upper strata of the social structure because they did not practice polytheism as a means to advance their social standing. Therefore the Jewish citizens were divided from the Gentile citizens.

From these descriptions of the ancient Corinthian society, we can discern that the Hellenistic way of life was characterized by social class divisions. As stated in chapter 1, Lakeland has a pervasive culture of division along social class lines too. Maybe your community looks similar to ancient Corinth?

Since Corinth and Lakeland are similar to each other, could the Corinthian church and LUMC be similar as well? Our next examination will be of the ancient Corinthian church.

The Corinthian Church and the Writing of 1 Corinthians

Within Corinth's divisive culture, Paul established the Christian church. Paul's Corinthian ministry is documented by Luke in Acts 18. According to Acts 18:1–2, Paul came to Corinth during his second missionary journey.

Paul attended the Jewish synagogue and testified about his belief in Jesus of Nazareth (Acts 18:4). The goal of Paul's preaching was to convince people to accept Jesus Christ as the Messiah (Acts 18:5). Luke informs us that some Jews opposed Paul, but many Gentiles listened and believed (Acts 18:7–11). With this positive reception by the Gentiles, Paul was able to establish the Christian church in Corinth. These Gentiles and believing Jews were accustomed to living within the social and religious divisions in Corinth. This blending of several cultures into a monotheistic worshipping church may increase the potential for syncretism within the Christian church. The potential for syncretism is multiplied by the pressures to be polytheistic to advance one's social and financial standing in the city. Syncretism is a combination of different forms of practicing faiths. For Paul, there was a bringing together of Jewish, Christian, and pagan religious beliefs. This provided fertile ground for conflict, which was contrary to the unity and nurturing environment that Paul preached.

For eighteen months, Paul remained in Corinth where he preached and taught about Christ (Acts 18:11). Paul remained in Corinth longer than any other city except Ephesus. Except for the account of being brought before the proconsul of Achaia, Acts provides no further information on Paul's ministry with the Corinthians. Luke notes the ministry of Apollos with the Corinthian Christians in Acts 18:24–28, but he does not reveal his knowledge of divisions within the Corinthian church.

In his absence from the churches he established, Paul desired to provide encouragement, teaching, and correction through letters that would be read to the various congregations. Like other Hellenistic letters, Paul's letters "extend his presence when he was unable to be present" (Collins, 3). Paul expressed this viewpoint when he writes in 1 Corinthians 5:3, "Though I am absent in body, I am present in spirit." These letters demonstrate Paul's apostolicity. Apostolicity is "a guard of ecclesial unity, because apostolicity is organic not merely formal. The fathers see apostolicity organically, as ecclesial growth literally from the Apostles themselves" (Cross). These letters help to maintain Paul's apostolic teachings within the churches he founded. It seemed that Paul intended for his churches to exercise unity among their members so that they could be successful in sharing the good news of Christ. He believed that unity could be achieved in the midst of the various religious beliefs that existed in Corinth and within the people who attended the Corinthian Christian church.

What prompted Paul to write the first letter to the Corinthians? While in Ephesus, Paul received reports of division from members of Chloe's household. Paul uses several Greek terms in 1 Corinthians to describe these divisions, including *eris* (1:11; 3:3), *phusioo* (4:19), *krino* (6:1), *hairesis* (11:19) and *akatastasia* (14:33).

Eris is translated as "dispute" or "quarrel." Paul is the only New Testament writer who uses this term. It is used to describe "disputes that endanger the Church" (Balz, NT:2054). *Phusioo* can be translated as "blown up, puffed up, or conceited." This term is used in "six occasions in 1 Corinthians." Paul uses this term to "throw light on the behavior of those who are still oriented toward the flesh" or "false teachings" (Balz, NT: 5448). Balz translates *krino* as "judge or used in conjunction with judgment." He indicates that this word is used "114 times in the New Testament with one-third in the Pauline letters" (Balz, NT: 2919). In 1 Corinthians, Paul seems to use this term as a warning "against human judging or the condemnation of others" (Balz, NT: 2919). *Hairesis* translates into "heresies, party, or dissension." Paul uses this term "in a derogatory manner to mean dissensions based on false teachings that threaten the Church's unity" (Balz, NT: 139). Balz translates *akatastasia* as "confusion, disorder, or tumult" (Balz, NT: 181). Paul used this derogatory term to show concern for threats to the church's unity.

All of these terms work together to show that there was a troubled situation in the Corinthian church. Paul must have felt this situation was so serious that he could not wait until his next visit to Corinth to personally address the church's disunity. He was compelled out of his concern for church unity to address the divisions and maintain his apostolicity in a letter to the Corinthian church.

What were the primary causes of the divisions? Paul alluded to three causes. First was the report on factions within the church. Chloe's people reported that arguments were based on attachments to a specific apostle, teacher, or Christ (1 Corinthians 1:11–12). Therefore the factions were divided among the followers of the teachings of Paul, Apollos, Cephas, and Christ. Paul does not provide any details on how the various factions disagreed with each other. Keener believes the Corinthian Christians favored specific teachers based on Corinth's divisive social context brought into the church by its members. "Thus higher-status members of the community seem to have preferred a more rhetorically skilled speaker like Apollos; and, sharing the values of their peers they hoped to reach with the gospel, they rejected manual labor as a suitable occupation for a moral teacher. Manual laborers in the church, however, appreciated a voluntarily lower-status, working teacher like Paul, even if his personal delivery in speeches left something to be desired of. In other words, the conflicting values of diverse groups in the broader society had been carried over into the church as divisive issues" (Keener, 1 Corinthians). No matter what the differences were among the various groups, the result was that the Corinthian church was being divided by its members.

The second cause is a previous letter that Paul wrote to the Corinthians. Paul references this letter in 1 Corinthians 5:9–13. This previous letter contained Paul's warning on associating with sexually immoral people outside the church, thus providing an argument against syncretism and immoral practices of pagan religions. Paul was also alluding to the generally accepted "Jewish view that Gentiles were sexually immoral" (Wiersbe, 1 Corinthians 5:9). This perception can be understood when viewed through the lens of polytheism. Gentile pagan worship generally included sexually immoral acts among its participants. Paul's concern was for the Corinthian Christians who still participated in these pagan rites. Through their participation, the Corinthian Christians condoned immorality that Christian doctrine sought to condemn. Condoning or condemning these pagan immoral practices caused the church people to be further divided.

The third cause is found in Paul's questions. The questions appear to be concerning marriage (7:1), meat sacrificed to idols (8:1), spiritual gifts (12:1), the contribution for the saints (16:1), and Apollos (16:12). The church could find itself further divided with the various sides on each of these subjects.

There are social and theological differences that divided the Corinthian church. The result of these differences was people not getting along with each other. The root issue seems to be that the people were self-centered. They focused on their own understandings and beliefs, which sometimes were contradictory to Paul's beliefs and proclamations. They were acting like people of the world instead of people of the Holy Spirit. Regardless of which side of the argument the Corinthians found themselves, they alienated each other with their arguments. This alienation, like today, caused people to run out through the church's revolving doors. These revolving doors caused the Corinthian church to be less effective in ministry than it could be because of the absence of the inactives.

The secular and religious context of 1 Corinthians is characterized by division along social and ecclesiological lines. LUMC and, I would venture to say, most churches find themselves in the same situation as the Corinthian church. In ancient times, as well as our current times, the divisions within churches result in alienated church members who escape out the revolving door. I discovered that most of these alienated members drop out of the church until something encourages them to return. If that something does not occur, then they remain separated from the body of Christ.

If the past and present social and ecclesial contexts are similar, then what can we learn from Paul's guidance to the Corinthian church to help us build personal relationships with these inactive people?

Unity in the Church

The causes of division discussed earlier provide a picture of Christians failing to demonstrate Christian love toward others. This failure resulted in the alienation of members within the Corinthian church. These unholy behaviors are unacceptable to Paul. Paul implies in 1 Corinthians that behaviors, ecclesiology, and theology are intimately linked to each other. Paul's goal for writing 1 Corinthians to the ekkleesía (1:2) was for them to be united in mind and purpose (1:10).

The 1 Corinthians letter contains many teachings in response to the messengers' report of division. Near the end of these teachings, Paul uses the human body as a similitude for unity (12:12–27). As a similitude, Paul uses the human body as a visible likeness of his vision of a healthy church.

Why did Paul use the human body to describe unity in the church? A simple reading would point out that this passage shows Paul's concern for the welfare of the members as they relate to each other within the church context. A healthy church is depicted as many members respecting each other while in ministry to each other and the world. Paul seems to use the human body as a physical comparison of how a healthy church can and should function.

One use of the human body similitude in Paul's time was describing unity among diverse social groups. "Paul's contemporaries who did this include Dio Chrysostom, Plato, Cicero, Seneca, Dionysius, Epictetus, Josephus, Philo, and Plutarch" (Collins, 458). When the human body is used, the writer typically makes "a plea for unity among the assembled community" (Collins, 460). Paul implies this view in this passage. Unity is needed for the church to fulfill its divine purpose in the world. Unity is possible if all members work together to maintain unity in their efforts to be the church that God desires. In order for the local church to achieve its divine purpose, it must have all of its members doing their part whereby the church's collective goal is obtained by achieving the individual goals together. Thus this perspective demonstrates the necessity for the local church to do what it can to draw inactives back to the church. The effectiveness of the church is derived from all of the body's parts doing what they are designed to do. Paul implies that each person has a divine purpose that only he or she can do. When that part is missing, then the body cannot and will not be successful in achieving God's calling and desire.

Another use of the human body similitude is to demonstrate how diversity is necessary for an organization to maintain unity. Paul shows that unity and diversity can coexist within the same organism. Unity is possible when diverse members are called by one God into one body with one Holy Spirit dwelling within them. Within this body, no one person, calling, or gift is greater than the others are. Paul urges unity by showing that all members are urged to work toward the common good of the whole body not for one member. Diversity of spiritual gifts focused on working together enables the church to accomplish its tasks, which results in effective ministries. Paul expressed this during his discussion on spiritual gifts (12:1–11). Paul reveals that God provides spiritual gifts to the members to help build up the body of Christ or the church (12:7). The members are different from each other in experiences, talents, and spiritual gifts. "Like the human body, the Body of Christ has a diversity of parts functioning together" as a united organization (Walvoord, 1 Corinthians 12:12). In 1 Corinthians, Paul implies that all members are necessary components of the body (12:22). Without the diverse members, the body could not exist (12:14). The local church needs all of the spiritual gifts working within its ministries so that the church is more effective in building up the body and sharing the gospel of Christ with others.

The last use of the human body similitude is to show the necessity of all members with their different roles. These church roles could have been defined by the spiritual gifts each person possessed. Paul points out that each member is important regardless of status. The *greater* and *lesser* members of the body have equal importance. With the absence of any members, the body is not able to function at its greatest efficiency. "Different parts are needed if a body is to exist. So too, no believer should think of himself or his gift as inferior and so desire another member's gift" (Walvoord, 1 Corinthians 12:14–20).

It seems that Paul believes that unity is achieved within a divided church when its members realize that it takes all of them to fulfill God's purpose. This realization empowers them to set aside their own self-centeredness to focus on the needs of others and those of the collective church. This focus is demonstrated when each member respects the other members regardless of status or spiritual gifts.

How is unity promoted within the church by different individual members? Paul indicates that the promotion of unity within the church begins when the members realize that they may be diverse but belong to one body (12:12–14). The diverse anatomical parts are arranged into one unit called the human body. These diverse parts work together so the whole body can perform its functions. These diverse parts, who are people united in the church, are brought together through one Spirit and one baptism (12:13). This baptism is the same for all members regardless of status, heritage, or citizenship (12:13).

Regardless of your position on baptism, Christian doctrine views baptism as the means to initiate a person into the church body. Baptism into one body becomes the divine equalizer making all people equal to each other in the sight of God. Beyond this, the members are to serve the church's common good in ministries that glorify God. The Holy Spirit helps these believers to grow in a continuous spiritual manner. Paul seems to imply that one of the tasks of the Holy Spirit is to help the members come to the understanding of the church as one body originated to serve God in a united manner.

Paul's discussion then turns toward showing mutual dependency among the diverse members (12:15–17, 21). The body cannot function effectively without the foot, the hand, the ear, the eye, the nose, or any other body part. The mutual dependency is shown in the task(s) that each body part is designed to perform. Each body part needs the other body parts for the human body to be as effective as it can be. The body parts cannot deny their own importance to the whole body (12:15–16) or the necessity of the other body parts (12:21–23).

The church resembles the human body in that each member mutually depends on the other church members for the church to be as fully effective as possible. It takes all of the members working together for the body to function. This means that church members continue to be a part of the church regardless of their degree of participation. Therefore the church needs all of its members to be successful in doing what God needs each church to do for the building up of God's kingdom. The church also needs visitors to it so that the members can encourage them through the sharing of their faith so that the visitors become committed church members.

Paul also infers that members are not to envy the position or gifts of other members. Each member has equal importance within the church. Regardless of status or gifts, every member is necessary "to the integrity or completeness of the whole" (Clarke, 1 Corinthians 12:12).

Unity is further promoted through God's equipping of the members. Paul discussed earlier in chapter 12 that spiritual gifts were distributed by God through the Holy Spirit according to the service and workings that the member was to perform (12:1–11). Paul reiterates that God is the One who places the members into the body at their proper place (12:18). The human body would not be the human body without all of its parts in their proper place. If all of the body parts were the same, there would be no body. The same can be said for the church. If everyone had the same gift or position, there would be no church because it could not exist when all of the members are alike. God formed the church with its various members possessing diverse gifts in such a way as to best convey harmony and unity. "A variety of talents and attainments in their proper places is as useful as are the various members of the human body" (Barnes, 1 Corinthians 12:18–19).

Unity is further promoted when the various members render respect and care to the other members (12:24–26). God provided the structure called the body of Christ. In God's eyes, all people are equal to each other. Paul shows that God arranges the church to produce unity and equality. Equality is demonstrated when respect is given to all people inside and outside the body. If members realize that they need the other people to be successful, then they may understand that each person has equal standing within the church. If the members understand that each has equal status, then the members may be able to see that their differences should not promote division but encourage unity.

Paul goes on to indicate that when the members see that each are equal in God's eyes and in their individual standing within the church, the members would render care to each other out of respect (12:26). This respect and care would be demonstrated through the intimate relationships among the members. "This was God's plan that members of the spiritual body would demonstrate a mutual concern for the well-being of others so that rivalry would cease and genuine unity would exist" (Walvoord, 1 Corinthians 12:21–26). Through these caring and nurturing relationships within the body, the members help each other grow in the grace and knowledge of Christ. Their mutual respect would promote unity and tear down the walls of division. Their social, ecclesial, and theological differences could be tolerated in these kinds of relationships so they do not become dividing walls within the body. John Calvin thought Paul meant this respect to be a duty carried out by Christians. "It is their duty … in being joined together in love and charity with one another, every one of them should bestow to the profit of all that which he has received, according as his ministry requires" (Calvin, 1 Corinthians 12:26).

Paul indicates that when the members embody Christ's teachings, they will be living as the body of Christ (12:27). This last verse brings us back to the conflict that exists within the church. The standards for Christian living are difficult to uphold while living in a pagan society. However Paul's teaching leans on the work of the Holy Spirit within the church to guide its members in living out their faith in a respectable manner. Paul believes the respectable manner is for each member to use their spiritual gifts to accomplish their divine purpose while rendering respect and care toward all people. If each member practices this belief, then the church can be united in providing effective ministry to its members and visitors within their social context. The intimate relationships among the diverse peoples could help the members accomplish their tasks and spiritually grow.

Unity can be achieved through the members. Unity can be obtained when the members use their different spiritual gifts to build up the church. The local church's edification can occur when the members relate at a high level where respect and care are rendered to each other. This rendering may help in developing and conducting ministry that uses the diverse spiritual gifts of the members. Within this kind of Christian community, the members would not use their social status or spiritual gifts as tools of division but as tools of compassion and nurture. In this kind of environment, the members can strive toward helping their church to grow as much as possible. The personal relationships among the members can also help in resolving future conflicts.

Unity can be achieved in the safe environment called the body of Christ. The church is a multifaceted organism with Christ as its head and believers as its parts. The church provides the means for its members to grow in knowledge of Christ while they serve God with their spiritual gifts. This growth is enhanced through the personal relationship of the individual members with God and others. These relationships help members "to function collectively as the Body" (Dunn, 60).

The church's purpose, as pursued by a unified group of believers, is extended when its members reach out to those outside the body. This shows that the church becomes nurturing as it shares its faith with those in the pagan society. This sharing includes inviting these people to attend worship. Following worship, the members are called to continue reaching out to them until they join the body.

Summary

Apostle Paul believes that the church can achieve unity, but it would require a tremendous effort by the members. It would require the church to provide the means for the members to serve God by using their spiritual gifts in ministry. It would also require the church to develop the means for the members to encourage each other through their participation within the church's ministries. This encouragement would be extended by the members with respect and care toward other members and those outside the Christian community. This encouragement could guide members toward growing in the grace and knowledge of Christ. This edification could also help members realize their dependence on each other for spiritual growth and the success of the collective church in accomplishing God's purposes. This mutual dependence can help the members unite to achieve this divine purpose.

According to the 1 Corinthians 12 human-body similitude, Paul thinks that believers can be united within the church in spite of their social and theological differences. The members can set aside these differences out of Christian love and respect. Christian love can enable members to edify each other and visitors with the goal of living up to the standard of Christian living proclaimed by Jesus Christ.

These scriptural insights help us see that God's intent for the body of Christ is to be composed of members who help each other grow and to reach out to those who are not believers in Christ. It can also be perceived that God expects the active members of the body to encourage the inactive members to return back to active participation so that the local churches can achieve the purposes that God designates for each one.

As a United Methodist, I will examine my denomination's dominant doctrine and polity in light of these newly developed scriptural insights in the next chapter. Regardless of denomination, most denominations have the same viewpoints as United Methodists with regard to church membership care and ministries. Please do not skip this next chapter if you are not United Methodist! You may be surprised at how close we are in our views!

Chapter 3

Theological Insights

John Wesley is the founder of Methodism. The UMC traces its heritage back to him, therefore Wesley's theology dominates Methodist doctrine and teachings. His teachings were designed to help people live out their faith in practical ways within the pagan societies they lived in.

John Wesley believed the local church can be a harmonious organization. This unity is possible through the relationship of church members to each other. These relationships can help the church to be more effective in ministry. We will study the Wesleyan theology of holiness to discern how the church can achieve unity through members' relationships.

John Wesley agrees with apostle Paul. Wesley believes that Christians are to live a life in the Spirit of God. This life is characterized by spiritual growth provided through the means of God's grace. Within the fellowship of the church, Christians are encouraged to use their spiritual gifts to edify each other and the church in ministry service. This edification is possible when believers strive to live a holy life. This Wesleyan theological approach is called a theology of holiness.

The present understanding of church membership in the UMC is rooted in Wesley's theology of holiness. It has evolved from the early Methodist Societies to its current practices. In this chapter, we explore an understanding of Wesley's theology of holiness. We will then look at the practice of this theology by the Methodist Societies and the present UMC. We will conclude with a discussion on church membership and the influence of church member inactivity.

John Wesley's Theology of Holiness

The overarching theme in John Wesley's theology is holiness enabled by the work of God's grace. In one of his sermons, Wesley explained holiness as "a love of God that teaches us to be blameless" and that "all of our thoughts, words, and actions are acceptable through Christ Jesus" (Wesley, *Sermons* "The New Birth").

To have an understanding of holiness, we will examine the distortion of the image of God and how God renews this image through Christ. We will conclude with some further thoughts of Wesley concerning the dimensions of holiness.

The Distortion of the Image of God

The creation story revealed that creation was in perfect harmony as seen through humanity's relationship with God. Wesley thought that holiness was expressed in this initial divine-human relationship as humanity pursued God's intended purposes.

God created humans in God's image possessing sense, understanding, and a will. "As such he was endued with understanding; with a will including various affections; and with liberty, a power of using them in a right or wrong manner, of choosing good or evil" (Wesley, *Sermons* "On the Fall of Man"). I believe that it was this divine image that enabled humanity to relate to God by responding to God's love with human love. This mutual love resulted in a good quality of life for humanity because of the power and presence of God.

God's image within humanity was distorted by disobedience toward God by eating the forbidden fruit from the tree of the knowledge of good and evil (Genesis 2:17). This first disobedient act toward God is commonly referred to as "original sin." This original sin corrupted the whole human nature by distorting God's image within humanity. It seems to me that humanity's decision to disrupt its personal relationship with God resulted in suspending the good quality of life enjoyed in Eden and in the presence of God.

Wesley believed that the image of God was not totally destroyed but was only damaged. With this distorted image of God, humanity "commenced [to be] unholy, foolish, and unhappy" (Wesley, *Sermons* "On the Fall of Man").

In several of his sermons, Wesley explained that the image of God within humanity consisted of three separate images, which are "natural, political, and moral" (Wesley, *Sermons* "The New Birth").

Natural Image: The natural image consists of endowments that make humanity capable of entering a relationship with God. This first image is composed of reason, will, and freedom.

Reason is "the conceiving a thing in the mind" and "comparing perceptions with each other" and "the progress of the mind from one judgment to another" (Wesley, *Sermons* "The Case of Reason Impartially Considered"). Therefore reason helps humans to discern order, enter into relationships, and make decisions.

Wesley understood will as "the desire that drives one toward certain life decisions" and freedom as "the liberty that one exercises to make choices, judgments, and discourses" (Wesley, *Sermons* "The End of Christ's Coming"). He thought will and freedom were inseparable. "Without freedom, both the will and the understanding would have been entirely useless" (Wesley, *Sermons* "The End of Christ's Coming").

Reason, will, and freedom derive their character from the quality of relationships that one chooses to enter. Wesley believed that we are "prone to evil" because we are "lovers of the world … [and] pleasure more than lovers of God" (Wesley, *Sermons* "The Righteousness of Faith"). Therefore humans use their freedom to choose to disobey God. This disobedience harms the individual by compelling him or her to replace the divine-human relationship with a corrupted sense that focuses on self instead of God. This self-focus guides people toward spiritual destinations that are contradictory to God's intended purpose.

Political Image: God gave this second image to humanity as the abilities of leadership and management. At creation, God granted humanity a position of privilege and responsibility as "the channel of conveyance" of order and harmony between God and the rest of creation (Wesley, *Sermons* "The General Deliverance").

Original sin resulted in humanity taking a self-serving perspective in its management of themselves and creation in ways that are contrary to God's intended purpose. Contradiction is manifested in self-pride and selfishness.

Moral Image: This last image provides humanity "with characteristics that are found in God, such as justice, mercy, and truth" (Wesley, *Sermons* "The New Birth"). Wesley thought that this is possible only in a right relationship with God where believers "receive and obey God" (Wesley, *Sermons* "The New Birth"). When individuals receive these spiritual traits directly from God, they also possess the responsibility of "communicating to others what they have received from God" (Wesley, *Sermons* "The New Birth"). This image enables humans to love God and others. Original sin caused humanity to set aside the divine-human relationship to pursue disobedience and moral ends that were not intended by God. Therefore humanity stopped reflecting God and began reflecting "the image of the devil" (Wesley, *Sermons* "The New Birth").

In order for humanity to be what God intended, God had to bring about a restoration of God's image within humanity through Jesus Christ.

Renewal of God's Image

Based on his perspective of humanity's fall, Wesley believed that humanity did not have a transforming capability within itself. Therefore humanity's spiritual restoration had to be accomplished by the Trinitarian God. God took the redeeming initiative to send Jesus Christ to humanity to teach humanity how to respond to God's redemptive actions. God sends the Holy Spirit to prompt humanity toward a divine-human relationship whereby God renews the divine image through holiness.

Wesley relied on Scripture for his perspective. His thoughts were based on a few Pauline passages: Colossians 3.10 ("being renewed in the image of God"), Romans 8.29 ("conform to the image of God"), and Philippians 2.5 ("having the mind of Christ"). Wesley believed that spiritual transformation was the "very heart of Christianity" where God can "renew our hearts in the image of God" (Wesley, *Sermons* "Original Sin").

The guiding force behind spiritual transformation is God's grace, which is "the root of all holiness" (Wesley, *Sermons* "The Witness of the Spirit"). Wesley believed that "everything in the Christian life comes from the grace of God in Christ" (Stokes, 37).

Grace can be defined as the freely offered gift of God's love that prompts individuals to demonstrate affection and obedience to God. Taking the initiative, God grants grace according to what each person spiritually needs. Grace helps people grow in the love and knowledge of God. Wesley believed that God provides three kinds of grace: prevenient grace, justifying grace, and sanctifying grace.

Prevenient Grace: Prevenient grace is God's "love that surrounds all humanity and precedes any and all of our conscious impulses" (Custer 59). According to John 3:16, God's prevenient grace is available to all people.

This grace prompts "our first wish to please God, our first glimmer of understanding concerning God's will, and our first slight transient conviction of having sinned" (Custer, 59). This grace enables "a far deeper and clearer conviction of inbred sin" as the Holy Spirit bears "witness with our spirit that our sins can be forgiven" (Wesley, *Sermons* "A Plain Account of Christian Perfection").

The goal of prevenient grace is to prompt unbelievers toward acknowledging their need for God. It continues to work in the lives of unbelievers until they respond positively toward repentance. After prevenient grace's goal has been achieved, justifying grace begins to work. However, there is no lapse of God's love as grace moves from prevenient to justifying.

Justifying Grace: Justifying grace's goal is to guide unbelievers toward entering into a personal relationship with God through Jesus Christ.

Repentance is the positive human response to God's conviction of sin. This response is manifested when people are guided by the Holy Spirit to express sorrow over their sins and realize that they cannot spiritually save themselves. This sorrow helps unbelievers turn toward God and enter into the divine-human relationship whereby holiness can be pursued. This sorrow includes the realization that they have endangered their souls by not having a relationship with God. After repentance, God guides the person through justification, propitiation, and regeneration, which occur simultaneously.

Justification is God's acceptance of the sinner by forgiving sins. Wesley explained justification as "not being cleared of the accusations of Satan, nor of the law, nor even of God" but the unbeliever receives "a pardon [or] forgiveness of sins … by faith" (Wesley, *Sermons* "Justification by Faith"). Faith, he writes, is "an extraordinary trust in God under the most difficult or dangerous circumstances" (Wesley, *Explanatory Notes* "1 Corinthians 12:9"). "Christian faith is not only an assent to the whole gospel of Christ, but also a full reliance on the blood of Christ; a trust in the merits of his life, death, and resurrection" (Wesley, *Sermons* "Salvation by Faith"). Therefore the new believer is saved by God's grace and responds with faith in God through Jesus Christ.

Propitiation, also known as atonement, was accomplished by Jesus Christ on the cross as a sacrifice for humanity's sins (1 John 2:2). Wesley described propitiation as Christ declaring "his righteousness for the remission of the sins that are past" which "God set forth through faith in his blood … As this occurs, there is therefore no condemnation now to them which believe in Christ Jesus" (Wesley, *Sermons* "Salvation by Faith"). Propitiation becomes a present reality for the individual when he or she expresses faith in God by accepting Christ as Lord and Savior.

The last spiritual action is regeneration, which is the renewal of the image of God within the new believer. This is also known as new birth because God causes the self-centered corrupted spiritual nature to cease and spiritually forms a new creation in Christ.

Through regeneration, God adopts the newly created saints into the family of God where they have eternal life as "joint heirs with Christ" (Romans 8:17). This adoption enables the indwelling of the Holy Spirit for guidance in making moral decisions and discerning God's will.

When all of these divine actions are completed, justifying grace transitions to sanctifying grace where God can do greater things in the believer's life.

Sanctifying Grace: Sanctifying grace is God's action to set believers apart from their pre-Christian selves. The results of sanctifying grace are changed behaviors and attitudes whereby believers can learn "how they ought to serve God and to be useful to their neighbor" (Wesley, *Journal* "In London Again").

Wesley's hope was that the love of neighbor would increase as the love for God grew. As these loves grew together, holiness would increase in the believer. If believers continue responding to God's grace by increasing in faith and pursuing God's will, then this image continues to be perfected by God. Sanctifying grace remains with believers in order to deepen the divine-human relationship whereby God can work toward a fully restored image within the individual.

It seems to me that the likelihood of possessing a fully restored image of God within this life does not seem possible. I am reminded that we "cannot be as holy as God" (2 Samuel 2:2). However Wesley believed that, through Christ, God can achieve what seems impossible by human standards (Matthew 19:26). I understand that God's expectation and calling for us is much higher than we believe that we can attain. It seems to me that if we let God increase in us and our selfishness decrease, then we are empowered by God to reflect the divine qualities of righteousness and love. I understand this to be Wesley's desired outcome of holiness.

Dimensions of Holiness

Wesley saw holiness in two dimensions, which are personal and social. These two dimensions are inseparable and interdependent on each other because of their presence within believers.

Personal holiness occurs throughout the individual's spiritual journey. God begins the restorative process at the individual level through "personal sanctification and salvation" as God helps us to "know ourselves by virtue of being born of God" (Wesley, *Sermons* "On the Holy Spirit").

Wesley believed that "works of piety" enhance believers' spiritual growth and helps to deepen the divine-human relationship (Stokes, 44). Wesley described works of piety as any means by which believers spiritually grow and improve their manner of relating to God and neighbor. His examples of works of piety included prayer, meditation, Bible study, and devotions.

Christianity is a social religion because God created people to be social beings relating to God and each other. Personal holiness leads toward social holiness because "Christianity … is essentially a social religion … that cannot subsist at all without society—without living and conversing with other men" (Wesley, *Sermons* "Upon Our Lord's Sermon on the Mount").

For Wesley, social holiness was the outward manifestation of the inner spiritual transformation. In essence, social holiness is the love of God resulting in the love of neighbor. Love of neighbor is where believers can combine spiritual faith with practical actions.

One way that Wesley thought believers showed love of neighbor was through sharing with others what they learned from God. The *others* can refer to unbelievers or fellow believers. Wesley believed that this kind of sharing helped promote spiritual growth for themselves and the others.

Social holiness was also demonstrated through works of piety and works of mercy, which are "typically conducted within the social context" (Stokes, 44). Social works of piety are the same as personal works of piety except they are practiced with others. Wesley expanded the list of social works of piety to include public worship, participation in Holy Communion, and fellowship. These works of piety also focus on individual spiritual growth. I believe that these works serve as a physical reminder of the power and presence of God. Through these reminders, we can reflect on the quality of life within the divine-human relationship. It seems to me that these reflections may encourage us to live out our personal fellowship with God through loving trust and obedient service to God.

As God helps us to "increase in love," we are empowered to "abound in love" for our neighbor (1 Thessalonians 3:12). Love of neighbor is expressed by believers through acts of mercy. Wesley defined works of mercy as any tangible deed that helps those in need. His examples of works of mercy included "feeding the hungry, clothing the naked, entertaining the stranger, visiting those that are in prison or sick, or … contribute in any manner to the saving of souls from death" (Wesley, *Sermons* "The Scripture Way to Salvation"). Through these acts of mercy, believers participate in God's redemptive work within humanity.

My experiences have shown that the needy neighbor is more receptive to the gospel message of Christ when physical and/or emotional needs are tended to first. The reality of holiness can be experienced by believers when they encounter the redeeming power of God through their service. Holiness is also experienced by the neighbor who encounters the caring presence of God through the acts of kindness.

Wesley thought that personal and social holiness helped believers to "see others through the eyes of Christ and therefore respond to the needs of others as Jesus did" (Stokes, 44).

Personal Relationships: Wesley recognized that personal relationships were important to one's spiritual growth. The effects of holiness are demonstrated within these personal relationships. Some common relationships that all believers have are with God, the church, and neighbors.

Wesley taught that the relationship with God compels believers toward relationships with others because the divine-human relationship "unites believers into one Body" (Wesley, *Explanatory Notes* "1 Corinthians 12:12–27"). Once people become believers within the faith community, they can begin to experience more of God's love. This union encourages believers to deepen "the love of God and of our neighbor for God's sake … not only for a time, but to the end" (Wesley, *Explanatory Notes* "1 Corinthians 13:4"). Therefore spiritual transformation can also lead to authentic personal relationships with one's neighbors who are inside and outside the church.

Wesley designed the Methodist Societies to cultivate personal relationships as God's grace empowered the society members to relate to each other in a nurturing manner. This caring manner may lead to a deeper level of trust that allows believers to hold each other accountable as they help each other strive for holy living.

My own spiritual journey began when someone invited me to join a faith community. Through that church's ministries, my faith was nurtured until I could make my own profession of faith. These relationships continue to encourage me to grow in God's grace and express my love of God through ministry. Therefore, for me, love of God and neighbor are key ingredients in my spiritual journey.

Meaningful personal relationships with other believers may lead toward greater Christian service. Wesley taught that God's love urges believers to "help … care … and serve others" (Wesley, *Explanatory Notes* "2 Corinthians 5:14"). This love of God and neighbor continues to grow because "the fire which burned in the apostle never says it is enough" (Wesley, *Explanatory Notes* "Philippians 1:9").

Summary: John Wesley's theology of holiness is the dominating theology within Methodism. The basis of this theology is Wesley's perspective on God's redeeming action following the fall of humanity.

The goal of God's redemptive actions is the restoration of the image of God in which humans were created.

The restorative work of God is accomplished through the various kinds of grace that help people pursue a life of increasing holiness. Wesley designed the Methodist Societies with the pursuit of holiness in mind.

Methodist Societies

In 1739, several people approached John Wesley with a desire to continue their spiritual growth outside the Anglican Church. Wesley's response was to establish small groups called Methodist Societies. The purpose of these societies was to "promote real holiness of heart and life" (Heitzenrater, 22).

Admission into these Methodist Societies required only "a desire to flee from the wrath to come and to be saved from their sins" (Wesley, *Sermons* "The Ministerial Office"). This desire exhibited a person's love of God. The society helped members to engage in a disciplined life of prayer, worship, service, and accountability. This pursuit enabled people to exhibit their love for God through their love for their neighbors.

General Rules

To help the societies' members pursue holiness, Wesley devised three general rules to promote "a life of personal holiness and morality" (Heitzenrater, 22). "Do no harm. Do good. Attend to the ordinances of God" (Wesley, *Sermons* "Upon Our Lord's Sermon on the Mount").

The first rule is "Do no harm." Wesley taught this rule by stating we are to live "in no outward sin" (Wesley, *Sermons* "Upon Our Lord's Sermon on the Mount"). Believers are encouraged to treat people in a nurturing and caring manner, which usually would be how they would like to be treated by others.

Wesley further preached that believers are to "avoid situations that may harm someone else" (Wesley, *Sermons* "Upon Our Lord's Sermon on the Mount"). He preached about profanity, drunkenness, slavery, and slander as avoidable situations because of their sinful, self-centered, and harmful nature. Christians were to reflect on the way their actions influenced others.

The second rule is "Do good." Good is produced by "acts of mercy to the body and the soul." Acts of mercy toward the body include "reaching out to the hungry, thirsty, naked, and imprisoned." Mercy toward the soul includes "helping people spiritually grow, including Bible study, accountability, and encouragement" (Wesley, *Sermons* "Upon Our Lord's Sermon on the Mount").

The last rule is "Attend to the ordinances of God." This rule reminded society members of the importance of active church participation. These ordinances included "fasting, private and public prayer, Holy Communion, Scripture reading, and public worship" (Wesley, *Sermons* "Upon Our Lord's Sermon on the Mount"). Through church participation, the society members were instructed on these ordinances and their importance to the pursuit of holiness. These ordinances, combined with the Methodist Societies' work, helped the society members participate with God in their spiritual transformation.

The group's general rules "were created not so much to monitor adherence to rules as to nurture a deeper love of God which members would manifest in the practice of Christian love in the world" (Frank, 46). Because Wesley believed in a practical theology, the group's structure encouraged its members to "not try to earn points with God but to enter more fully into a life of love—love of God and neighbor" (Frank, 46). The members were drawn deeper into this life of love through the weekly meetings.

Weekly Class Meeting

The Methodist Societies were divided into groups of eight to twelve people called classes. The society members attended weekly class meetings where they would hold each other accountable for "being Christians inwardly and outwardly" (Frank, 47). Wesley believed there were several benefits to attending the weekly class meetings, which included "happy experience [of the] Christian fellowship," "bearing one another's burdens," "caring for each other," "a more intimate acquaintance with each other," and "edifying themselves in love" (Wesley, *Works* 8:254).

The class meeting began with the members greeting each other in Christian love. The class leader would open the class meeting with prayer. After the opening prayer, the class leader would conduct the accountability examination. The class leader would "carefully inquire how every soul in his class prospers, not only how each person observes the outward Rules, but how he grows in the knowledge and love of God" (Wesley, *Works* 8:301). "The point of this questioning was not to drive people out but to draw them to walk closely with God" (Frank, 47). The answers to these questions provided topics for instruction by the class leader. This instruction was to be encouraging in banishing the common ignorance of the Christian faith through "reproof and correction" (Wesley, *Sermons* "The Ministerial Office"). "If the common ignorance were banished, and every shop and every house busied in speaking of the word and works of God; surely God would dwell in our habitations and make us his delight" (Wesley, *Works* 8:304). This instruction included how Christian doctrines could be expressed in the class members' outward manifestations of holiness. After the lesson, the class would enter into a time of intentional prayer, which allowed class members to ask God for forgiveness and guidance in living their lives. This prayer time ended with the class leader encouraging the members to pray for each other by "standing in the gap against the overflowing of ungodliness" (Wesley, *Sermons* "The Means of Grace").

The weekly class meetings not only endeavored to bring members closer to God, but they helped members to be in ministry with each other. This nurturing ministry guided members toward "proper Christian behaviors as the members pursued holiness" (Heitzenrater, 118).

During the weekly meetings, the members were able to build personal relationships with each other as "they came to know each other" (Heitzenrater, 119). As these relationships grew, the members were able to "extend the personal touch of discipline" (Heitzenrater, 118). Therefore personal relationships helped believers toward holiness.

Wesley's theology of holiness and Methodist Societies structure appeared to have been helpful in guiding people toward holy living. How does the current UMC's polity reflect Wesley's understanding of holiness?

Current United Methodist Polity

The UMC polity is found in *The Book of Discipline of the United Methodist Church*. This polity generally reflects Wesley's theology and seeks ways to adhere to Wesley's design to practice holiness.

The design of the Methodist Societies was so instrumental to the Methodist movement that it has been published in each *Book of Discipline* since the UMC unification in 1968. It seems that the expectation of the UMC is that its current members and local churches work in much the same way as the Methodist Societies.

Current perspective is that this theology of holiness is a "practical divinity [for] the implementation of genuine Christianity in the lives of believers" (UMC *Discipline*, 45). Let us look at current polity as it relates to the renewal of God's image, holiness, church membership, and local church responsibilities.

Renewal of God's Image

Current polity generally reflects Wesley's position on God's renewal of the divine image. However, there are some updates for contemporary times.

The first of these ways is that the genuine Christian life is possible by "living in a covenant of grace under the Lordship of Jesus Christ" (UMC *Discipline,* 41). This covenant expresses God's love working in, through, and for the believers' edification. It seems to me that this covenant is expressed spiritually as love of God and outwardly as love of neighbor.

For this covenant to be fully realized, divine grace is "required to renew our fallen nature" (UMC *Discipline,* 46). Humanity cannot repair its fallen nature because "we are never accounted righteous before God through our works or merit" but God can redeem us because of "faith in our Lord Jesus Christ" (UMC *Discipline,* 69).

Current polity expresses Wesley's perspective on the salvation process. Conversion is defined as "the righting of relationships by God through Christ," which "calls forth our faith and trust as we experience regeneration by which we are made new creatures in Christ" (UMC *Discipline,* 46). After conversion to faith in God, regeneration and new birth follow.

Regeneration and new birth are expressed as "the renewal of man in righteousness through Jesus Christ, by the power of the Holy Spirit, whereby we are made partakers of the divine nature and experience newness of life. By this new birth the believer becomes reconciled to God and is enabled to serve him with the will and the affections" (UMC *Discipline*, 69).

After this renewal occurs, the Christian experience is marked by "personal transformation expressed as faith working by love" (UMC *Discipline*, 46). God causes personal transformation, which results in "a heart habitually filled with the love of God and neighbor and having the mind of Christ [whereby] God's grace and human activity work together in the relationship of faith and good works" (UMC *Discipline*, 47).

Entire sanctification, which is also known as Christian perfection, is "a state of perfect love, righteousness and true holiness … and should be sought earnestly by every child of God" (UMC *Discipline*, 69). I feel that this is a bold goal for each Christian. It seems to me to be problematic because it does not inform us as to how we can know we have attained this perfected state. However ambiguous this notion appears, I believe that it provides the lifelong motivation for believers to be in a state of continual improvement of their relationship with God and neighbor.

I sense that, as one goes through life, there may be an ebb and flow in the restorative process as demonstrated in our inward attitudes and outward actions. UMC polity hopes that Methodists will rely on God as they endeavor to have more of the mind of Christ.

Personal and Social Holiness

In Wesley's theology, personal and social holiness overlap each other. Within the *Book of Discipline,* there is little overlap because the main emphasis of polity is on social holiness.

Personal holiness is stressed as "faith and love put into practice" by individual Methodist Christians (UMC *Discipline*, 45). The polity does not provide any further guidance. Current polity moves quickly to social holiness with language of incorporation of the believer "into the United Methodist Church as the community of believers" (UMC *Discipline*, 45). Methodists are expected to express their "response and discipline" to God's grace through "Christian mission and service [whereby] love of God is always linked with love of neighbor" (UMC *Discipline,* 47).

The *Book of Discipline* emphasizes God's actions and underscores the human response. It implies that the faith community is a vital part of the Christian's pursuit of holiness. Therefore the expectation is that Methodists are to be active in their local churches. "The communal forms of holiness in the Wesleyan tradition not only promote personal growth, but also equip and mobilize for mission and service to the world" (UMC *Discipline,* 48). As Wesley believed, current polity shows the interdependence of personal and social holiness.

With holiness as its guiding theology, the *Book of Discipline* conveys the expectations of discipline that assumes "accountability to the community of faith by those who claim that community's support" (UMC *Discipline,* 49).

Wesley's perspective on holiness provides the theological foundation for Methodists. Current UMC polity by and large reflects Wesleyan theology. It also guides Methodists on pursuing holiness through the church membership vow.

Church Membership Vow

One of the encouragements to pursue holiness that all UM Christians encounter is the church membership vow. In order to be members of the UMC, individuals vow to be loyal to Christ through the UMC "with their prayers, presence, gifts, service, and witness" (UMC *Discipline,* 143).

"Primary responsibility and initiative to fulfill these membership vows rest with each member" (UMC *Discipline,* 149). Current polity does not elaborate on what is expected in prayers, presence, gifts, service, and witness. However, polity does provide some principles which Methodists can apply to their pursuit of holiness. The principles are discipleship, mutual responsibility, personal ministry, and accountability.

Discipleship is defined as "personal growth and the developing of a deeper commitment to the grace of God," which is possible through "prayer, worship, the Sacraments, study of Scripture, Christian action, systematic giving, and growing in appreciation of Christ" (UMC *Discipline,* 143). Discipleship is enhanced through mutual responsibility.

Mutual responsibility is "the obligation to participate in the corporate life of the congregation with fellow members." Members voluntarily enter into a sacred covenant with God and the UMC in which they "shoulder the burdens, share the risks, and celebrate the joys" (UMC *Discipline,* 143). Mutual responsibility is expressed through personal ministry.

Personal ministry occurs when members "share in the ministry committed to the whole Church of Jesus Christ." Members become "servants of Christ in mission in the local and worldwide community" (UMC *Discipline,* 143).

The last principle of accountability helps Methodists better apply the first three principles. Members are ultimately accountable to God, but also they are to hold each other accountable "for their faithfulness to the covenant" (UMC *Discipline,* 144).

Each Methodist is expected to fulfill the membership vow. The responsibilities outlined below express the importance of the local church in helping Methodists to meet these expectations.

Local Church Responsibilities

The local church is defined as a group of members "seeking the power of godliness, united in order to pray together, to receive the word of exhortation, and to watch over one another in love, that they may help each other to work out their salvation" (UMC *Discipline,* 72). "The church, under the guidance of the Holy Spirit, is to help people accept and confess Jesus Christ as Lord and Savior and to live their daily lives in light of their relationship with God" (UMC *Discipline,* 133). The local church is charged with providing "for the maintenance of worship, the edification of believers, and the redemption of the world" (UMC *Discipline,* 21) by organizing itself for "the nurturing and serving function of Christian fellowship" (UMC *Discipline,* 47). Therefore church members are empowered through the local church to "move from general Christian principles to specific actions" of faith (UMC *Discipline,* 48). To guide the local church toward achieving these responsibilities, current polity provides further guidance.

With regard to church membership vow, the local church begins its responsibility before one makes a decision to join. This responsibility is fulfilled as the church prepares individuals for membership through confirmation and membership classes. These Christian education endeavors inform one of membership responsibilities and expectations.

In response to the membership vow, the local UM congregation vows to help "increase their faith, confirm their hope, and perfect them in love … that leads to life eternal" (UMC *Worship,* 109). The local church's role is to provide structures in which its members may exercise their faith. Furthermore, "The local church shall endeavor to enlist each member in activities for spiritual growth and in participation in the services and ministries of the Church and its organizations" (UMC *Discipline,* 149). The primary goal of the local church's ministries is individual spiritual growth. Spiritual growth is pursued through several corporate avenues, including "worship … and study [designed] to connect faith and daily living, and continually to aid the members to keep their vows" (UMC *Discipline,* 149).

The local church has an obligation to minister with all of its members. The obligation to minister to inactive members is expressly described: "Active members and the pastor are to minister to members in an effort to enable the members to faithfully perform the membership vows and covenant" (UMC *Discipline,* 144). The local church is to "encourage members to return and to assume the [membership] vows" (UMC *Discipline,* 144). "The church has a moral and spiritual obligation to nurture its nonparticipating and indifferent members and to lead them into an active church relationship" (UMC *Discipline,* 149). The lay leadership is to "reenlist the [inactive] member in the active fellowship of the church" (UMC *Discipline* 150). The church's leadership is to encourage the inactive member to make a decision in regard to one of four things: "(a) reaffirm the baptismal vows and return to living in the [faith] community; (b) request transfer to another United Methodist church where the member will return to living in the [faith] community; (c) arrange transfer to a particular church of another denomination, or (d) request withdrawal" (UMC *Discipline,* 150). Therefore current polity expects the local church to have a ministry with inactive members. My pastoral experiences show that most churches do not.

It appears to me that current polity expresses the desire for inactive members to return to the faith community where they can continue their spiritual growth. Implied in this desire is the need of the church for the inactive members so that the local church can have a better opportunity of fulfilling God's will.

Current Methodist polity generally agrees with Wesley's theology with some modifications to its practice. For a brief overview of the thinking of some contemporary Wesleyan theologians, see appendix A.

The Influence of Inactivity

Inactive members cannot meet the membership expectations as detailed by UMC polity. However, this does not provide enough detail as to the negative influence of inactivity. The effects of inactivity influences individual spiritual growth and church unity.

Individual Spiritual Growth

The apparent influence of inactivity is on the potential for spiritual growth. The church, through its ministries, enhances the believers' spiritual growth. Spiritual growth is limited when inactive members choose to separate themselves from the local church's ministries.

Inactive members are not helped by the faith community in growing in the grace and knowledge of Christ. The increase in divine knowledge includes understanding the will of God for the individual. This discernment process is derailed without the church's involvement. The inactive members are less able to know what their spiritual gifts are or how God is calling them to use those gifts. Continued hindrance to Christian education may also lead inactive members toward little or no congregational expressions of love for God and neighbor through ministry service. Thus inactive members are not serving God or neighbor as they might. As Wesley feared, this lack of ministry may demonstrate unbelief or lack of trust in God.

Church Unity

UMC members are united with each other and God through Jesus Christ. This union seeks for church members to help each other spiritually grow through the church's ministries. Unity emphasizes the mutual dependency of the members on God and each other, which is hindered by inactivity in three ways.

The first hindrance is to the ability to serve. Lack of participation renders inactive members less than effective in serving God and others with their spiritual gifts through the church's ministries. Their absence prohibits them from gaining an understanding of the church's common good and how they can help promote that common good.

The second hindrance is to the church's overall effectiveness. This achievement is partially fulfilled when church members pursue holiness in the church's ministries through works of piety and mercy. The church is less effective in achieving God's will because of the absence of inactive members.

The last hindrance is in the relationship building that takes place among church members. The church's ministries help its members to strive for holiness. As these ministries are conducted, relationship building may also be occurring. These relationships cannot be built or improved when inactive members are not present.

The local church must reach out to inactive members. The local church is to love inactive members, as Christ loves them, and work toward building relationships with them in hope of their return to active participation in the church.

Summary

The insights gained in this chapter impress upon me the power and presence of God within the life of the believer and the church. This divine presence is continually active within humanity to guide believers toward achieving God's purposes by loving God and neighbors.

The insights of this chapter compel me toward inactive member ministry. I have discerned that this is the direction that God is guiding LUMC and me. Beginning as work on our church health, the church's direction has evolved into a caring ministry with our inactive members. Our hope is that all of us will spiritually grow as we pursue holiness together.

Chapter 4

The Caring Ministry

This chapter provides the method and methodology for implementing a caring ministry with inactive members. The overview section is comprised of the limitations, key terms, goals, and hypotheses. The method section has the details for a phased implementation plan for the caring ministry. The ministry's methodologies will be surveyed in the methodology section.

Overview of the Ministry

The caring ministry helps active members to build authentic personal relationships with inactive members. The desire for this ministry is to help members nurture and care for others through personal relationships. The first step that the LUMC lay leadership wanted to begin with was a visitation ministry with inactive members. This blossomed into the development of this caring ministry. In a later chapter we will look at how to expand this ministry to include all church members and worship visitors.

Limitations

The ministry focus is on relationship building with others. Most church growth theories do not address this issue of working with inactive members, except to indicate that limited resources should not be used to reach them. These theories cite the large amount of effort and limited success as the reasons that inactive member ministries should not be pursued.

We have seen in previous chapters that inactive members are *still* members of the body of Christ and our churches. We have also learned from Scripture that the church's members are also to help the body to continue growing. The hope is that all members will be active church participants. However this would be in a perfected world of believers pursuing God's grace.

This caring ministry is not about numerical growth in church membership or worship attendance. Increases in these areas may result because of this ministry. It is important to keep in mind that the ministry's main goal is relationship building.

Key Terms

There are several terms to be defined before moving forward. The terms are caring ministry, inactive members, authentic personal contacts, formal contacts, informal contacts, active participation, Lay Advisory Committee, and directed interviews.

Caring Ministry: A caring ministry is a ministry where laypeople rebuild or reestablish relationships with inactive members.

Inactive Members: Inactive members are church members who have been absent from the Sunday morning worship service for more than twenty-four weeks.

Authentic Personal Contacts: Personal contacts are visits, written letters, or telephone conversations. These personal contacts are authentic when the inactive members or volunteers believe a relationship has been reestablished and/or improved.

Formal and Informal Contacts: Formal contacts occur during the ministry-structured visits on Tuesday nights. Informal contacts are interactive opportunities that occur outside the ministry structure at locations, such as the grocery store, bank, and post office.

Active Participation: Active participation is demonstrated when members participate in any activity or ministry sponsored by LUMC.

Lay Advisory Committee: This committee consists of three pastor-selected and pastor-trained church members who served on the Church Health Team mentioned in chapter 1. The responsibilities of this committee include being participant-observers, designing an introductory letter with response card, conducting and evaluating directed interviews, providing guidance, and assisting during the assessments.

Directed Interviews: A directed interview is a structured interview consisting of probing questions. These interviews are intended to result in narrative stories revealing perceptions about the visits with regard to relationship building between volunteers and inactive members.

Learning Goals

When LUMC implemented this ministry, we developed six learning goals that we used to evaluate this caring ministry and its impact with inactive members. The primary and overarching learning goal is to discover how a caring ministry consisting of prayer, telephone contacts, letters, and visits can be effective in rebuilding relationships with inactive members. The secondary goals correspond to the various communication methods used, which are prayer, telephonic communications, written communications, and visits. The newly intended future is for active members to rebuild authentic personal relationships with inactive members.

These learning goals will be assessed through directed interviews. Volunteers will provide immediate feedback on their formal and informal visits through directed interviews conducted on their individual ministry nights. Within two weeks of the formal visit, a directed interview will be conducted with the inactive members by the Lay Advisory Committee.

During the LUMC implementation, we included an assessment to determine the effectiveness of this ministry. These two assessments were performed by the Lay Advisory Committee. From these assessments, the Lay Advisory Committee made some changes to the caring ministry. The most dramatic change was the inclusion of caring for active church members and visitors.

Hypotheses

The Lay Advisory Committee began with a set of hypotheses that expressed its hope for the success of this new ministry. These hypotheses will be evaluated in the same manner as the learning goals.

1. Some learning goals will be achieved.
2. Some inactive members will return to active church participation.
3. We will rebuild positive relationships with 10 percent of the inactive members.
4. 50 percent of inactive members will not want any contact from the church.
5. Less than 10 percent of active members will volunteer for the caring ministry.

Method

This caring ministry was implemented in order to correct the way we were approaching our inactive members. The result was the implementation of a caring ministry with inactive members. The ministry's core features are personal contacts through prayer, writing, telephone conversations, and face-to-face visits. There are five implementation phases for this ministry, which are volunteer recruitment, volunteer training, inactive member selection, ministry implementation, and evaluation.

This ministry is significant because all Christian churches have difficulty staying connected to inactive members. This ministry is designed to help pastors and churches to engage in relationship building as one way in which to share the love of God with other people.

Team Structure

The caring ministry occurs in a structure composed of the pastor, the Lay Advisory Committee, and the weekly ministry teams. Details on this organizational structure are found in appendix B.

Pastor: The pastor will provide the primary leadership as an ex officio member of the Lay Advisory Committee. With the assistance of the Lay

Advisory Committee, the pastor oversees all aspects of the ministry as a participant-observer. As a member of the Lay Advisory Committee, the pastor ensures that the caring ministry's ownership resides with the laity and not in the office of pastor. This helps the ministry to continue into the future regardless of pastoral transitions. The presence and participation of the pastor impresses upon the congregation the importance of this ministry in the life of the church.

Lay Advisory Committee: This committee was defined earlier in this chapter. It provides the necessary lay leadership for this ministry. The committee members will serve alongside other volunteers as participant-observers. With the pastor, they will determine the ministry team meeting time(s), the target group of inactive members and visitors, and the volunteer recruitment goal. They also serve as consultants for these ministry teams during ministry implementation and assessment. This committee is also responsible for reporting to the church's main leadership body on the progress, success, and direction of the ministry.

Ministry Teams: Active church members will be recruited to fill four ministry teams that correspond to the week of the month. Team #1 will meet during the first week of the month. Team #2 will meet during the second week of the month, and so on up to Team #4. Each ministry team consists of at least seven volunteers. This size allows each ministry team to have three visitation groups and a team captain. The more people recruited into the ministry teams will result in more visits being conducted. The size of these ministry teams can be smaller, but it would result in very limited results and success. Doing this ministry on a monthly basis instead of weekly would enable inactive members to sever their relationship with the church in between the ministry nights.

The team captain remains at the church to address issues that arise with the visitation groups, to pray, to collect the completed visitation report forms, and to assist with the directed interviews. The ministry teams meet on their assigned ministry night for only two hours, thus the volunteers are asked to commit to two hours of ministry each month or twenty-four total hours of ministry in the year! Visitation groups will endeavor to conduct two visits on each assigned night. Prior to the assigned ministry teams' night, the visitation groups will arrange an appointment with the inactive members for the formal visits. This appointment making is not necessary with visitors.

Volunteer Recruitment Phase

This phase's objective is to recruit enough volunteers to fill each ministry team. Volunteer recruitment will occur primarily at the church. Enrollment invitation will occur after each presentation and worship service. Volunteer recruitment will occur through bulletin announcements, worship service appeals, and small-group presentations. This phase will be conducted for four weeks.

The volunteer recruitment goal for LUMC was twenty-eight people. Four volunteers will be team captains while the remaining volunteers will compose the visitation groups. The LUMC Lay Advisory Committee chose Tuesday night as the ministry night because this night had the fewest conflicts with other church and community events. This is an important step in that you want the night that will afford the largest potential volunteer pool as possible.

When they enroll, volunteers will select a specific ministry night (or week if you want to view it as that) of the month that best fits their schedules. The volunteer enrollment form can be found in appendix C.

The bulletin announcements will appear in each church bulletin for one month. These announcements emphasize relationship building among members, improvement of our church's health, and the scriptural mandate for the nurturing within the body of Christ. These bulletin announcements are in appendix D.

The lay members on the Lay Advisory Committee will make the pulpit appeals during the Sunday morning worship services. These pulpit announcements will be personalized by the speaker. The general content of these appeals includes ministry intent, reasons to volunteer, and enrollment instructions. After the worship service, the speaker for that worship service will staff the enrollment table to answer any questions and to enroll volunteers. Sample pulpit announcements can be found in appendix F.

Presentations will be made to several church small groups. The Lay Advisory Committee with assistance by the pastor will develop a presentation schedule to include all adult and youth small groups within the church.

The ministry will be presented to all adult and youth Sunday School classes, the men's and women's groups, the youth group, and other church small groups, such as prayer groups, Bible study groups, and accountability groups. These presentations will occur during the regular meeting of each of these groups. See appendix E for the group presentation.

Volunteer Training Phase

After the volunteer enrollment phase is complete, the volunteer training begins. Volunteer training will occur during each ministry team's assigned ministry night over a period of three months. The training is divided into three two-hour sessions. The training goal is to prepare the volunteers to pray, call, and visit the inactive members. Each volunteer will receive a training manual that will be produced by the Lay Advisory Committee. This training handbook contains all of the topics that will be covered during the training. This training handbook is found in appendix G. The slideshow presentations that will be used during the training can be found in appendix I.

First Training Session

The first training session provides the ministry's framework. This framework consists of avenues of contact, church member viewpoints, and relationship building.

Avenues of Contact: The avenues of contact are in-reach, out-reach, hands-on, and prayer. In-reach occurs when the ministry focuses on active and inactive church members. Outreach is possible with the ministry working with visitors who are outside the church membership. Hands-on is possible when volunteers put their faith into action by participating in this practical ministry. Prayer helps volunteers rely on God, and less on their own understandings, for direction before, during, and after their visits.

Church Member Viewpoints: For relationship building to occur, volunteers will need to possess positive viewpoints about inactive members. This part of the training focuses on inactive members because of the negativism that surrounds inactive members. Through a discussion on perceptions, volunteers can recognize negative viewpoints they may have about inactive members. This recognition helps volunteers understand how they may affect the inactive members' desires to return to the church. It provides the means for volunteers to identify these negative perceptions and begin to transform their attitudes before encountering the inactive members.

Relationship Building: Relationship building is possible if the volunteers desire to see others spiritually grow. This training helps focus the volunteers on building relationships by putting others first. This focus is demonstrated when volunteers take interest in the needs of others and work on winning someone else's trust. The volunteers are asked to use their informal contacts to continue building relationships outside the structured ministry night.

Second Training Session

The second training session focuses on relationship building, listening skills, role-playing, and confidentiality. This session is also contained in the team members' training handbook. This session begins with a review of the first training session.

Relationship Building: We will begin with a review of the viewpoints of active and inactive members. The volunteers begin to build relationships with each other through an exercise of introductions. Another exercise of sharing personal perceptions about the church will conclude this portion. appendix H contains the exercise forms that will be used for this training portion.

Listening Skills: The volunteers will begin to use listening skills in the relationship building training in this session. This training portion will help volunteers understand how to use listening skills in this ministry.

Role-Playing: With the classes on relationship building and listening skills behind them, the volunteers will put their newly acquired skills into practice in role-playing scenarios. This exercise simulates possible positive and negative scenarios that volunteers may encounter during their contacts. This training allows the volunteers to exercise their skills within a controlled environment so that all volunteers present are able to learn from each other. During this exercise, volunteers will receive specific guidance to enhance their skills whereby they become more comfortable with face-to-face visits. The role-playing scenarios are found in appendix J.

Confidentiality: We do not know what the volunteers will encounter when they visit with inactive members. They must understand that they should not share any information gained during these visits or during the debriefing sessions at the end of the ministry night with anyone. Sharing personal information outside the caring ministry could adversely affect relationship building with the inactive members. Confidentiality is a mandate for trust to grow. Trust is needed for relationships to be reestablished.

Third Training Session

The third training session focuses on building upon the skills acquired during the second training through role-playing, and concludes with a re-emphasis on confidentiality. The agenda schedule of this session needs to include each ministry team selecting the inactive members that their respective teams will be working with. How each team will do this is discussed below. This session is not in the team members' training handbook because it includes a multitude of role-playing scenarios. The basics for this ministry are included in the team member's training handbook. The role-playing and confidentiality discussion simply reiterate what has already been taught.

These three training sessions will prepare the volunteers for contacting active members, inactive members, and visitors. The Lay Advisory Committee remains available for additional training and issue clarification during ministry implementation and execution.

Inactive Member Selection Phase

LUMC possessed a computerized membership program that works in conjunction with worship attendance tracking. If your church does not possess such a tracking system, then you will need to procure one or develop a tracking system that allows you to know the number of absences for all church members.

LUMC identified forty-eight inactive members living locally within its church membership. Other inactive members lived outside the geographical area of effective pastoral coverage. Depending on your denominational and/or church position with people living outside the pastoral coverage area, you will need to determine a course of action for these inactive members. I will not cover this in this book because of the wide variety of methods to deal with this issue.

The main function of this task is to identify inactive members who live locally. This task also determines regular visitors who will be contacted to invite for church membership. Therefore you can probably see how a computer program for membership tracking is very helpful to make this caring ministry more effective and efficient than doing manual tracking. Although manual tracking is possible, my recommendation is to leverage technology for this ministry.

After identifying the inactive members with whom the ministry teams will work with, the identified inactive members will be contacted with an introductory letter. The introductory letter explains the church lay and clergy leaders' desire to rebuild relationships with them. The introductory letter is found in appendix L.

When LUMC did this ministry, we constructed this introductory letter inviting them to participate by responding via a self-addressed stamped postcard indicating their desire. We found that very few, if any, would use the response card because of the severed relationship with the church. Therefore we recommend including all of your local inactive members into this caring ministry. However, if you deem it necessary to include a response card, I have provided the one we used in appendix M.

During the third meeting of each ministry team, which is the last training session, the ministry team members will select their team captains, the makeup of the visitation groups, and the inactive members with whom they will minister. This will take about thirty minutes to accomplish. The first task for the ministry teams during this particular meeting is to decide the composition of their visitation groups. This selection will also designate who will serve as team captain. The visitation groups consist of no fewer than two adults and no more than three people. Earlier you saw that we are inviting youth members (middle and high school students) to participate.

These youth volunteers will work with two adults on a visitation group, but cannot serve as a team captain.

Afterward, each ministry team will use a list of available inactive members to make their selections. This availability list may generate discussions about the inactive members. When the inactive member selections are complete, each visitation group will use this list to perform two tasks. The first task occurs before and after the formal visit. This task is to pray for God to guide them as they approach the inactive members. This prayer will be to offer thanks for the inactive members, ask God to open the hearts of the inactive members, and to calm the fears of the ministry team. The second task is to be achieved after the formal visit, which is to continue building relationships with the inactive members through informal contacts that arise through their everyday living events.

Ministry Implementation Phase

After the training and selection phases are completed, the implementation phase begins. The implementation phase occurs each ministry night. When LUMC started this ministry, the Lay Advisory Committee set a research period of four months after the training phase was complete. This amount of time was selected so that the ministry teams would have enough time to make the formal visits with inactive members and continue nurturing these new relationships through the informal contacts.

The first task in this phase is for the visitation groups to schedule an in-home formal visit with the participating inactive members. This telephone conversation is to last no longer than what is necessary to schedule the in-home visit. This telephone conversation starts the relationship building with the inactive members.

The prayer portion of this ministry occurs daily. The volunteers are asked to pray daily for inactive members. On the ministry night, the team captain will pray while the visitation groups conduct their visits.

The visitation groups will visit in the homes of the inactive members. These formal visits will last between fifteen and sixty minutes depending on the receptivity of the inactive member and the direction of the conversation. This formal visit provides volunteers with the opportunity to demonstrate their concern and compassion for inactive members. It helps the inactive members and volunteers to connect with each other on a personal level. After this first formal visit, the volunteers are encouraged to improve their relationships with the inactive members through informal contacts.

Evaluation Phase

The evaluation phase is conducted during the entire ministry implementation phase. The evaluation of this project is based on directed interviews, visit summaries, and observations.

During the first three phases, the Lay Advisory Committee will use directed interview questions with volunteers and inactive members. These directed interviews will result in narratives that will be evaluated. These narrative evaluations enable the Lay Advisory Committee to assess the effectiveness of the ministry.

During the ministry implementation phase, directed interviews with the volunteers will be conducted at the end of each ministry night. The volunteers will give their perception about relationship building through debriefing, directed interviews, and visitation report forms. The visitation report forms found in appendix N will guide the volunteers in reporting the events of the formal visits and informal contacts. The directed interview questions with the volunteers are found in appendix O.

Within two weeks of the first formal visit, the Lay Advisory Committee will schedule a directed interview with the inactive member(s). At the end of the implementation period, another appointment will be scheduled with the inactive members to follow up. These interviews can be conducted in person or telephonically. These interviews help capture the perceptions of the inactive members on relationship building pursued during the formal visits and informal contacts. These interviews also help determine the effectiveness of the ministry. They can be another means for the church to continue cultivating the relationships with the inactives. The interview questions are found in appendix P.

The evaluation phase was expanded when LUMC implemented this new ministry. The narrative evaluations from the directed interviews were used in conducting the assessments. The Lay Advisory Committee conducted an assessment at the conclusion of the implementation period to determine ministry effectiveness. Another assessment was conducted one month after the test period conclusion to determine any modifications to the caring ministry. Discoveries from these assessments are incorporated in chapter 5 to discuss the expansion to active church members and visitors.

Method Summary

The method of design is a phased implementation plan that allows for sufficient recruitment, training, and evaluation time. The ministry and evaluation phases are flexible enough to allow for unforeseen circumstances. The method of evaluation allows relationship building to be evaluated through narratives.

Methodology

The methodology for this project begins with the scriptural and theological insights from chapters 2 and 3. The methodology of design and evaluation will be discussed in this section through a review of relevant literature. This methodology allows you to understand the foundational work for this ministry. The works of L. Charles Gray, Gerhard Knutson, and John Savage contribute to the project's design. Works of Carl Savage and William Presnell guide the project's evaluations.

Survey of Method of Design Literature

L. Charles Gray wrote *Reaching the Drop Out Church Member* for the Black Presbyterians for Renewal and Growth in 1982. He provides the reasons to develop a caring ministry for inactive members. In addition to the reasons that were garnered from Herb Miller, as stated in chapter 1, Gray's insights help us understand why church members become inactive.

Gray believes church members cease active participation because of anxiety. He identifies four kinds of anxiety common within the church setting: reality anxiety, neurotic anxiety, moral anxiety, and existential anxiety. Miller's reasons can be categorized into these anxieties. Reality anxiety occurs when "one's own personal history produces pain or a sense of disequilibrium" (Gray, 10). Examples of reality anxiety are failure to acknowledge all people associated with a successful ministry and failure to respond in a personal way when a church member falls ill. Neurotic anxiety occurs when a person's "thought patterns produce feelings not based on facts" (Gray, 11). An example of neurotic anxiety is a person believing that whispering people are talking about him or her. Moral anxiety is present when "one feels guilty because his/her behavior does not conform to his/her beliefs" (Gray, 11). Moral anxiety is present when people know they are not living up to the moral standards expressed in the church. Existential anxiety is exhibited when a person "is anxious about the meaning or lack of it in his/her life" (Gray, 11). This usually occurs as people get older and/or near the end of their lives.

Unresolved anxiety will eventually result in anger. According to Gray, "Anger is a response to anxiety and is always object-directed. In a church setting, it may be directed toward the pastor, a church member, or church staff member" (Gray, 9). "Unless listened to, the active member undergoes behavior changes that are manifested in reduced churchgoing, reduced committee work, and a crisis of faith" (Gray, 11). When we combine this thought with Miller's reasons, we see that one event can extend into anxiety and into anger if not addressed within a short period of time. Gray believes anxiety-driven behavioral changes are exhibited over six to eight weeks. If no pastoral or congregational care is provided within that timeframe, the church member will likely become inactive. "Dropping out is a way of coping," he suggests. "The dropouts are persons who have been hurt and are still hurting" (Gray, 12).

Gray asks a vital question about inactive members: "How does the Church constructively reach out in love and understanding to the inactive church member?" (Gray, 12). He does not propose any possible resolutions to this question. However it is a question that this ministry must take into account.

Gerhard Knutson, in his 1979 book titled *Ministry to Inactives*, suggests ways to reach out to our inactive members. His insights guided the volunteer training development. Knutson provides the motivation for this ministry.

The caring friend is present for the other person regardless of what may happen in the external world. Caring means ... being present for one another. From experience, we know that those who care for us become present to us. When they listen, they listen to us. When they speak, they speak to us. And when they ask questions, we know that it is for our sake and not for their own. Their presence is a healing presence because they accept us on our terms, and they encourage us to take our own life seriously and to trust our own vocation (Knutson, 10).

To express care, Knutson encourages readers to look at their perceptions about inactive members. "The active people in the congregation often attribute certain names to or develop certain feelings toward inactive persons. These feelings and names represent barriers, labels, and stereotypes" (Knutson, 12). He suggests that "ministry to the inactives begins by overcoming certain attitudes and names in order that the energy and love of the gospel may rightly and lovingly motivate us" (Knutson, 13).

This ministry goal influences volunteer recruitment. "The recruitment process involves looking for people who have gifts in relating to and caring about others" (Knutson, 35). He points out that training builds up the confidence of the volunteers in their abilities. Training builds skills through "practice conversations" when they can "share with another person" and "deal with issues" (Knutson, 36).

These caring persons willing to share God's love compose the visitation groups. "The [groups] go out two by two with one another's support" (Knutson, 37). Visiting is easier when the members support each other. As the groups continue visiting with the inactive member, they help "renew the bonds of fellowship and friendship" (Knutson, 37).

John S. Savage has completed the most work in the area of inactive-member ministry. He has written two books on this subject: *The Apathetic and Bored Church Member* and *Listening and Caring Skills in Ministry*.

Savage agrees with Gray on anxiety and anger being the forces that cause inactive members to distance themselves from the church. He believes the "anxiety-anger complex" results in "helplessness, hopelessness, apathy, and boredom" (Savage *Apathetic*, 5–6). Savage believes relationship building is the key to help inactive members come back to active church participation.

Savage's insights helped in developing our volunteer training. The training helps the volunteers make "meaningful contact in a ministry of caring, and develop their human responsibility to each other and God" (Savage *Apathetic*, 72). His training model involves "orientation to the ministry," "sharing," "listening skills," and "relationship building" (Savage *Apathetic*, 74).

Training focuses on developing and using listening skills. The use of listening skills is to check the inactive members' perceptions about the church and the visits. Savage writes, "The perception check is a caring behavior" (Savage *Listening*, 39). By listening and responding in a positive way, the volunteer is attempting to connect personally with the inactive member. "By identifying emotionally with the speaker's feelings, you convey caring and sensitivity to the person's inner emotional condition" (Savage *Listening*, 39).

The intent of listening skills is to hear the stories of inactive members. "Storytelling is a form of self-disclosure," according to Savage (Savage *Listening*, 77). By allowing inactive members to tell their stories of hurt and anger and disappointment and abandonment, the volunteers are working "more diligently on getting in touch" with inactive members (Savage *Listening*, 77). Through these stories, the volunteers may be able "to discern the deeper truth" about why the inactive member walked out of the revolving church door (Savage *Listening*, 79). If we understand the deeper truth, volunteers may be able to develop a meaningful relationship with the inactive member through sympathy and empathy. This understanding empowers the volunteers with thoughts about how to invite and encourage the inactive back to active church participation.

In summary, these authors provide many insights into the design of our inactive-member ministry. These insights include identifying perceptions, listening skills, and volunteer training.

Survey of Method of Evaluation Literature

The caring ministry focuses on relationship building. Relationships cannot be quantified through empirical or scientific data. The way to evaluate relationship building is through narratives. Carl Savage and William Presnell, in *Narrative Research in Ministry*, propose an evaluation method called "the process of narrative analysis" (Savage and Presnell, 74).

Narrative Evaluation: Analysis begins when the volunteer "attains a grasp of the ways in which the researcher's own story intersects with the narrative of concern" (Savage and Presnell, 74). The ability to evoke a true story starts with the influences of our own lives. As volunteers attain self-awareness, they become a "story broker" and a "handler of people's stories" (Savage and Presnell, 76). The story broker "draws out multiple narratives that intersect around a concern or opportunity" (Savage and Presnell, 75). In the caring ministry, inactive members' stories surround the multifaceted reason for their church inactivity. Volunteers draw these stories out to determine how effectively the church is responding to them through the caring ministry. In order to provide accurate feedback on these stories, volunteers must be aware of their "preconceptions, interpretations, or presumptions" (Savage and Presnell, 76). This ministry allows volunteers and inactive members to reveal their stories to each other.

The narrative stories occur when people "share a human experience" (Savage and Presnell, 81). The human experience provides the means to receive "self-defining narratives" of inactive members and look for how these narratives "intersect with the larger [congregational] narratives" (Savage and Presnell, 81). This intersection enables the volunteers to intimately connect with inactive members, thus providing the opportunity to deepen their relationship. A deeper relationship enables an invitation to be extended to the inactive member.

To capture these narratives, we will be conducting intentional interviewing during this ministry. This type of interviewing "not only reports experience" but "also reveal[s] the meanings by which they have been formed as people and the relationships they have with each other" (Savage and Presnell, 83). The most effective method to capture experience and meanings is called the ethnographic method. This method is where "the researcher becomes a participant-observer as a listener" (Savage and Presnell, 108). This method enables the researcher to examine "relationship encounters" (Savage and Presnell, 109). As evaluators of the ministry, the Lay Advisory Committee members serve as the researchers. The best means to capture an evaluation of this ministry is by the Lay Advisory Committee members participating as members of the weekly ministry teams.

Savage and Presnell explain there are two parts to evaluating narratives: observing change and discerning transformation. Observing change is possible when one "compare[s] the context before and after the new ministry intervention" (Savage and Presnell, 124). Discerning transformation occurs when a "marked change toward a preferred future" (Savage and Presnell, 124) exists. This kind of evaluation enables the Lay Advisory Committee to determine the effectiveness of the ministry, but also to detect things that need to be modified to fit into their particular church.

Methodology Summary

The project's design methodology is derived from several sources. There are few scholarly works available on inactive-member ministry. However, the available literature does provide insights contributing to the development and implementation of this caring ministry.

The approach to the ministry's evaluation is a new development based on narratives. This evaluation method is important because empirical data cannot be obtained on relationship building.

Chapter 5

What Happened

This was a groundbreaking ministry for LUMC because there was no existing visitation ministry or ministry with inactive members. The ministry implementation consisted of Lay Advisory Committee selection, volunteer recruitment, volunteer training, inactive member selection, and field research. This chapter focuses on what happened when we first implemented this new ministry.

The Lay Advisory Committee

This ministry began with the church clergy and lay leadership identifying this ministry as a priority, which was detailed in chapter 1. After this determination, the pastor invited three church members to serve on the Lay Advisory Committee. These people served on the Church Health Team when the priorities for our Church Health Action Plan were established. These individuals clearly demonstrated their desire to see the church's health improve through their participation during the Church Health Action Plan process. All three accepted the invitation.

Before ministry implementation, the pastor and the committee members determined the work of the Lay Advisory Committee. They established the following committee responsibilities:

1. Serve as participant-observers during the ministry;
2. Consult with the pastor during the ministry;
3. Assist the pastor in designing an introductory letter with response card;

4. Determine the ministry team meeting time and meeting structure;
5. Determine the target group of inactive members;
6. Set the volunteer recruitment goal;
7. Help conduct and evaluate directed interviews; and
8. Assist in ministry assessments.

The working relationship of this committee with the pastor was very positive. They were not intimidated by the presence of the pastor, which was demonstrated by their frankness. They were extremely honest with each other and the pastor in their observations. They were not afraid to discuss openly different options available to overcome the setbacks to ministry implementation. This allowed the committee to work toward developing and maintaining an effective inactive-member ministry. These observations clearly indicated that the right people were chosen for this arduous task.

During its meetings, this leadership group detailed its responsibilities for ministry implementation, established the team meeting time, developed the volunteer recruitment plan with recruitment goals, designed the introductory letter, and determined the target group of inactive members. The committee's responsibilities, detailed in chapter 3, were fulfilled well.

One responsibility that was not previously stated, but assumed by the committee, was the arrangement of pulpit or church appeals. This committee determined that the pastor should present the first appeal, which was conducted on the first Sunday of the enrollment month. The three lay members conducted the other appeals on the other three weeks of the enrollment month.

During implementation, this committee's lay members faithfully served as participant-observers. They attended their respective assigned week without fail. They provided a leadership and church health perspective within the weekly visitation groups. During the directed interviews with the volunteers, each committee member contributed personal insights that helped the weekly teams work toward improving this ministry. These personal insights included mannerisms, body language, possible conversation starters, and conversational language.

At the end of our research, this committee facilitated an assessment session with the volunteers. They evaluated the directed interviews of the volunteers and the inactive members.

This committee worked as designed in chapter 3. Their calmness and determination to correct an issue was valuable to the inner working of this ministry. Overall, the Lay Advisory Committee provided valuable leadership and contributed significantly to ministry implementation.

Volunteer Recruitment Phase

Volunteer recruitment began shortly after the work of the Lay Advisory Committee was completed. Recruitment was conducted through bulletin announcements, pulpit or church appeals, and small-group presentations. This phase lasted for one month. The recruitment goal was twenty-eight volunteers, of which four would become team captains and the remainder became team members.

The bulletin announcements provided advance notice of the new ministry. The announcements contained a brief description of this ministry and enrollment instructions. Details of these bulletin announcements are found in appendix D. There were no inquiries from these announcements; thus no volunteers were recruited through this method.

The lay pulpit appeals were somewhat effective. As planned, the pastor and the Lay Advisory Committee members conducted these announcements. They understood the intended goals of the ministry because of their involvement in the ministry planning process. This understanding enabled the presenters to provide enthusiasm for the ministry and relate the ministry toward improving the church's health. During these announcements, the presenters explained volunteers' tasks and the requested length of their commitment. The presenters staffed the enrollment table following the worship services. These pulpit announcements are detailed in appendix F. This method resulted in 32.1 percent of the total volunteer enrollment (nine of the twenty-eight volunteers).

The group presentation was the most effective recruitment technique utilized as indicated by the number of participants enrolled into the ministry. The pastor conducted these group presentations because of his availability and attendance with most of the groups. The effectiveness was facilitated by the opportunity for the audience to ask questions about the ministry. The group presentation slideshow is located in appendix E. Nineteen people enrolled through this technique, which was 67.9 percent of the total volunteer enrollment of twenty-eight volunteers.

The enrollment form had several purposes. The first purpose was for volunteers to select the week of the month that best fit their busy schedules. The second purpose was to identify volunteers willing to serve as team captains. These achieved purposes led to the assignment of the volunteers to the week they signed up for and decreased the effort to find individual team leadership. This enrollment form is found in appendix C.

Twenty-eight volunteers enrolled. The volunteers were structured as detailed in chapter 3 and appendix B. With a goal of this ministry to care for inactive members, the Lay Advisory Committee thought that the word *CARE* should be used to name the weekly teams. Therefore the names of the teams are C, A, R, and E. The volunteer recruitment resulted in the C Team having a team captain and nine volunteers. A Team had a team captain and five volunteers. R Team enrolled seven volunteers, but no team captain. E Team had one team captain and four volunteers.

After determining that the volunteer recruitment goal originally established was not met, the ministry leadership decided that a revised plan must be developed so the visitation ministry could still be conducted with a reduced number of volunteers. The Lay Advisory Committee asked the pastor to serve as the team captain for the R Team, which did not have a team captain. With a reduced number of volunteers in two of the weekly teams, the Lay Advisory Committee realized that more time would be needed for those teams to conduct their formal visits. The other change to the ministry's plan was to allow the team captain to serve on a visitation group instead of remaining at the church to resolve issues. However, this would not apply to the C Team. This revised plan brought a minimal risk of the team captain not being present for problem resolution and prayer. This risk was further reduced when all team captains volunteered to use their personal cellular phone to resolve any issues that arose. With this change, the leadership deemed this as an acceptable and reasonable risk.

Volunteer Training Phase

The volunteer training was divided into two sessions. These sessions lasted two hours each. These sessions were conducted when each team met on its assigned night. The teams took two months to complete the training. There were no absences during each team's training sessions. The pastor conducted these training sessions. The Team Member Handbook and visual training slideshow helped to facilitate the training. The handbook can be found in appendix G. The slideshow is in appendix I.

The first training session's objective was to provide a framework for the volunteers to conduct the ministry. This session consisted of a lecture ending with a question-and-answer period. The topics covered were avenues of contact, church member viewpoints, and relationship building. This session's agenda was conducted in accordance with the design in chapter 3.

The volunteers were asked to participate during the first training session by reflecting on how they could apply the lecture topics to this particular ministry. There was little reaction from the volunteers during the training until the discussion on viewpoints and relationship building. The discussion on viewpoints exposed hidden perceptions that had never been a part of an exchange among these team members. The revelation of these viewpoints was manifested in head nods and acknowledging comments, such as "I do that." This exposure helped them look at how destructive these perceptions could be to building positive relationships with inactive members. One volunteer commented to a Lay Advisory Committee member that he did not realize how hurtful his perceptions were to his relationships with other church members.

The viewpoint discussion was followed by relationship building. This topic sequence was developed to help the volunteers see how their perceptions enhanced or hindered their ability to build personal relationships. One volunteer stated, "If we are to be successful in gaining the trust of the inactive members, then positive viewpoints about them would help us work harder to build relationships with inactive members."

At the conclusion of this first session, the volunteers were asked if this training session had prepared them to make visits and build authentic relationships with inactive members. Most volunteers acknowledged that they were not fully prepared to accomplish these tasks. The consensus was that the first session sparked their interest and helped prepare them for the next training session.

The second session's objective was to provide practical application of the training in a safe environment where all volunteers could learn from each other. This session's agenda was a review of relationship building followed by instruction on listening skills. After the listening skills instruction, the volunteers applied the lessons through role-playing. The final block of instruction was on confidentiality.

All of the volunteers actively participated in this session. The different scenarios for the role-playing provided real-world situations that volunteers could encounter. These scenarios can be found in appendix J. The volunteers learned from each other by seeing their fellow volunteers handle various situations on their own. The volunteers stated in the question-and-answer time that the role-playing gave them confidence and helped overcome their anxiety for making personal contacts. Only one volunteer stated that she was not fully ready yet. The other volunteers agreed that they were more ready after this session because of the practical application of relationship building, listening skills, and perspectives. Group consensus also revealed that most of the volunteers still possessed some apprehension to visiting, but not enough to stop them from going out.

Inactive Member Selection Phase

This phase began after the Lay Advisory Committee meetings with the identification of inactive members through our church membership computer program. This program identified forty-eight local inactive members. There were more inactive members identified, but it was determined that they were outside the geographical area that our ministry could realistically impact.

An introductory letter with response card was mailed to these forty-eight members. This introductory letter is in appendix L. They were asked to respond by using the self-addressed and stamped response card within two weeks. A copy of the response card can be found in appendix M. At the end of the two-week response period, thirteen people opted out of the ministry through the return of the response card. One person requested a visit with the pastor, which resulted in the person telling his story of his inactivity and eventually opting out of the ministry.

We did not receive any positive responses to the letters. This lack of response was indicative that the inactive members were not willing to be participants in this ministry. The leadership determined that the remaining thirty-five inactive members who did not respond to the letter were the ministry's target population.

After the completion of the training sessions, the implementation process led each team to select inactive members to contact and begin to work toward building positive relationships. The C, A, and R teams chose nine members each. The E Team chose eight inactive members. A summary of the selection is found in appendix K.

During the selection process, all team members contributed to the discussion on the inactive members. These discussions resulted in the members having a better picture of each inactive member. The members talked about family backgrounds, community connections, vocations, and potential reasons for their becoming inactive. Each team was able to decide which inactive members to be in ministry with. These decisions were primarily based on mutual connections of one or more team members to the inactive members or to the inactive members' extended families.

After the teams made their selections, the volunteer training topics were reviewed. This review ended with another question-and-answer period. The lack of questions from the volunteers prompted the pastor to ask the team members some questions.

The first question was this: "How has this training and the selection process prepared you for this ministry?" The majority of the members responded positively on the benefits of the training. The same member who was not ready at the end of the training sessions was still not confident in her abilities to visit. She said, "It is good that we do not have to visit by ourselves." This prompted the reminder that all visits were to be conducted by at least two team members.

"Has the role-playing and working with each other during the past three months helped or hindered your confidence in the abilities of your fellow members?" The consensus of each team was that the training helped them to have confidence in themselves and in the other team members. There were no negative comments to this question.

The volunteers were excited to be a part of a new ministry when asked to reflect on visiting with inactive members. One member commented, "This ministry will help us overcome the reputation of being an unwelcoming church." This statement led to other positive comments about overcoming other stigmas about the church. Another member stated that this ministry could improve the church's health.

The teams ended this phase on a positive note. With the exception of one member, the volunteers seemed ready to begin the next phase of the ministry.

Ministry Implementation and Evaluation Phases

The objective of this phase was to build relationships with inactive members through telephone calls and visits. The teams reported on these efforts through directed interviews. A summary of these volunteer interviews is found in appendix O. The inactive members provided another perspective through directed interviews. A summary of the interviews with inactive members can be found appendix P. This phase, which lasted four months, consisted of telephone calls, formal visits, informal visits, and prayers. A results summary of this project is found in appendix K.

The individual visitation groups were required to make an appointment via telephone. Through the calling process, the teams identified five members who had moved out of the local area. An additional nine inactive members opted out of being visited during the telephone contact. This reduced the project's inactive member target population to twenty-one.

Two inactive members refused a visit when a visitation group made a cold contact visit after several unsuccessful contact attempts. This further reduced the ministry's inactive population to nineteen people.

During this phase, the C Team did not participate in the ministry. The C Team members attended both training sessions and indicated they understood what was being asked of them. However, none of the members returned to actually conduct this ministry during the four-month test period. The Lay Advisory Committee followed up on these members individually. One team member had been moved into a long-term care facility for health reasons and another one had become physically incapable of walking. They discovered that most of the team's volunteers were not committed to the ministry as they were to other nonchurch activities. They seemed confident in their skills to conduct visits with inactive members but indicated during the interviews that they did not want to visit people who were strangers to them. One team member confessed, "I just cannot bring myself to visiting strangers. I know that they are church members, but most of those people are still strangers to me."

This caused the ministry leadership to redistribute the C Team's inactive members among the other three teams. This caused a lapse in time between the introductory letter and the actual first telephone contact. During a directed interview, one of these inactive members commented, "I thought the church forgot about me because it was several months before I received a phone call after getting the letter. I thought that it was just another thing that the church did not follow through with."

When asked if the telephone calls developed authentic relationships, the volunteers concurred that they did not. When asked why not, they typically responded that the calls provided the means to lead to the formal visit but were not long enough to develop any kind of meaningful relationship. One team member remarked that the phone call was long enough to develop a superficial relationship for the task of setting an appointment.

The interviewed inactive members agreed with this observation. They were appreciative of the calls from their fellow church members but could not label these connections as relationships. One inactive member commented, "I have seen the church start a number of ministries to reach out to others, but they never materialize. I received the letter but did not respond because the church would not follow through again. Therefore I was very surprised to receive a phone call from a church member instead of the pastor. It was then that I realized that the church was serious in wanting to reconnect with me."

The scheduled first visit with the inactive members is called a formal visit. It is formal because of scheduling an appointment for a home visit. All nineteen remaining inactive members were visited. The visitation groups were generally received in a hospitable manner by the inactive members. The teams did not report any negative receptions by the inactive members. One team member reported that the appointment making contributed to warm receptions.

The visitation groups reported beneficial visits. The narrative summaries of the volunteers can be found in appendix O. Generally, the teams reported hesitancy by the inactive members to commit to returning to active church participation. We discovered that this hesitancy was generally due to the length of time away from the church. Most of the inactive members mentioned embarrassment to return to church after being away from the church for a lengthy time. However, most of them said that they would consider returning to church.

One visitation group discovered an inactive member was actively participating in the life of the church in a midweek Bible study but was not able to attend the Sunday worship services because of his employment. This visit indicated the need to track attendance at other church activities other than Sunday morning worship and to redefine who could be classified as an inactive member.

The teams discovered several reasons for inactivity. One commented that there were church members who did not want him in the church. This member's reluctance may also be connected to his length of inactivity, which the member reported to being over thirty years. Nine inactive members indicated that their inactivity was due to their vocation. Two people commented that their priority on the weekends was visiting their grandchildren in another state. One inactive member indicated that he had several personal problems that caused him to be inactive. Another member told the visitation group that family issues were taking his time on the weekends. Two members confessed that they were not putting any effort into being in church since they had moved away from their parents. One member did not indicate any reason. One member stated that she was too emotionally distraught over her family not coming to church, which caused her not to return to active church participation.

The visitation groups encountered a variety of reasons for inactivity, causing them to deal with each inactive member differently. Even the most cited reason (employment) had to be handled differently by the visitation groups because of the way the inactive members view their employment in connection to church attendance. The sharing of the situations during their ministry night debriefing helped others with future visits.

Were relationships built? See the overview of these results in appendix K. The directed interviews with the volunteers after the formal visits revealed that some relationships were established. Appendix O provides the summary of these interviews. The volunteers believed that nine relationships (47.4 percent of the nineteen visited inactive members) were established. The perceptions of the volunteers were very positive about the ministry. Most of the volunteers concurred that these relationships could result in those inactive members returning to active church participation.

Our interviewers discovered that twelve inactive members (63.2 percent of the nineteen visited inactive members) thought that a relationship was established with them during the formal visits. The summary of these interviews can be seen in appendix P. The inactive members were positive about the visits and this new caring ministry. Many inactive members believed that this ministry might draw them back to active church participation. The visits helped the inactive members to realize that they were still church members. Several inactive members commented that the visits caused them to reexamine their reasons for not being active in the church's life.

When asked if they would come back to active church participation, the majority of the inactive members were noncommittal. One member stated that he would not be back into the church until his own funeral. One other member stated that her reluctance to return was based on the many years she had been inactive. Although noncommittal, most of the inactive members did not rule out coming back to church.

After the formal visits, the volunteers were asked to seek informal contacts with their assigned inactive members. This was not as easy to do as the ministry leadership thought it would be. Each month the volunteers were interviewed to determine the quantity and quality of the inactive contacts. With a small town, the leadership thought that chance contacts would occur on a daily, and at worse weekly, basis. The ministry summary in appendix K shows the results with each of the inactive members. Of the nineteen visited inactive members, the visitation groups informally contacted eleven. These contacts were made at the local bank, post office, grocery store, and restaurants. When these contacts were made, the volunteers felt that they were successful in improving the relationships they had established during the formal visits. The volunteers believed that the informal contacts helped them to be successful in building relationships with eleven inactive members (57.9 percent of the nineteen visited members).

When interviewed, the inactive members overwhelmingly agreed that the formal visit opened the door for a relationship to be developed. However, they clearly indicated that the continued informal contacts in the local community helped to grow these relationships. One inactive member commented, "I thought that we would see the church people only once and they would be through with us. However, those two women talked to me each time they saw me, no matter where they saw me. I saw that these two people were serious in caring about me. I thought that if these two are this serious, could everyone else be too?" The number of inactive members who believed these informal contacts help build a positive relationship with them grew from twelve to fourteen (73.7 percent of the nineteen inactive members).

Because of these visits, four inactive members returned to active church participation. Three people have been active in worship attendance by attending at least one Sunday morning worship service each month after the formal visit was conducted with them. One inactive member was determined not inactive with his active participation in the midweek Bible studies.

The volunteers were asked to pray for the inactive members during the test period. The volunteers reported that they did pray for them. Most of the volunteers admitted that they did not pray for them daily but prayed at least weekly for them. The surprising result was with the weekly teams who had inactive members who had moved out of the local area. Our interviews found that the teams continued to pray for these particular inactive members too.

One volunteer stated that his visitation group prayed when they got into the car to go to their formal visits. This prayer calmed their nerves and helped them to focus on the tasks they were to perform. This same volunteer stated that they also prayed after the visit. He commented that the visits and praying helped him on his spiritual journey.

The volunteers concurred that prayer helped them overcome their fears of visiting. They also felt that prayer helped them to gain a positive view of inactive members. This change helped them to build relationships with the inactive members because it helped them not to give up on the inactive members.

During their directed interviews, the inactive members were told that the volunteers were praying for them. Most of the inactive members reacted with surprise. One inactive member asked, "Why should they be praying for me? I am not attending church, so who am I to them?" When told that the volunteers were concerned for him, he began to cry and appeared to be surprised at this concern.

When asked how this information made them feel, most of the inactive members indicated they felt embarrassed. One inactive member commented, "I am embarrassed that someone is praying for me while I am not praying for them. It kind of makes you feel very humble that strangers are taking time to lift you up to God!"

During the assessment interviews, there were no significant changes to the perceptions of the volunteers or inactive members.

At the end of the research period, the Lay Advisory Committee hosted a social event for the volunteers. The purpose of this event was to reveal the findings of the test period. The volunteers were excited about the findings. They expressed that they did not expect anyone to return to active church participation. However, they were mostly willing to continue participating in the ministry. The exciting part of this social gathering was the group's commitment to continue this ministry with some modifications. The Lay Advisory Committee inquired if the volunteers had thought of any changes that could be implemented if they continued to have this ministry. These changes are reflected in chapter 6 in the section "What Would I Do Differently." With the commitment of these volunteers, our church continued with this ministry in its expanded format.

Summary

The implementation of this project was stimulating. The Lay Advisory Committee helped to develop, implement, and lead a new ministry in the church. The volunteers served as God's instruments of caring love through their visits, calls, and prayers. The inactive members were able to experience authentic relationships based on God's love and human concern in which the door to return to active church participation was opened for them. They experienced the power of prayer that was being offered on their behalf in spite of their lack of church participation. Those inactive members who have returned to active church participation have the opportunity to enjoy the continuation of their spiritual growth and pursuit of holiness. The pastor gained confidence in lay people as he saw them sharing God's love with others in a caring and compassionate manner.

The results with the inactive members were promising. Of the original forty-eight identified inactive members, nineteen were visited (39.6 percent of the forty-eight). Fourteen inactive members (29.2 percent of the forty-eight) believed that relationships had been built with them. Four inactive members (8.3 percent of the forty-eight) returned to active church participation. The inactive members' perceptions were changed to see that active members were praying for them and cared for them in spite of their absence.

The results with volunteers were promising. Twenty-eight volunteers enrolled in this new ministry. Three of the four weekly teams were active in accomplishing their responsibilities. Throughout the duration of this ministry, the perceptions discovered during the training were changed. The volunteers now look at inactive members as church members who have been away from worship under a variety of reasons, but are still to be cared for by those who are active because they are still children of God within the body of Christ.

The work of the ministry leadership was accomplished mainly as designed. The unforeseen situation of an entire team not conducting the ministry caused the leadership to develop and implement a contingency plan that caused a delay for the inactive members between the introductory letter and the formal visit. The shared leadership roles between the pastor and laity could be extended into other ministries that extend God's love toward others who are on the periphery of the faith community.

This ministry was developed and implemented based on the perceived need of the active church members that was clearly established during the Church Health Action Plan process. The work on the church's health led to this need becoming a priority for a new ministry.

After the research period was over, the leadership team assembled the volunteers to provide the findings of the test period. After the findings were discussed, the Lay Advisory Committee asked the volunteers if this ministry should be continued. The volunteers were emphatic about continuing this ministry. Some modifications to the ministry were discussed. A decision was made that the ministry be modified to include church members who are absent from worship less than six months. One volunteer stated, "We need to catch people early while they are still active so that we do not have any long-term inactive members. If we care for them now, they will not become inactive later."

The final decision was made to continue this ministry with modifications into the future under complete lay leadership with minimal pastoral guidance.

Chapter 6

What Was Learned

This was a groundbreaking ministry for LUMC. How effective was it? What did I learn from this project? How did this project change me? What are some possible implications resulting from this project?

Brief Overview

The project's genesis is traced back to the decision by the LUMC lay leadership to work on its church health through the Natural Church Development process. The result was a Church Health Action Plan that placed inactive member visitation as a ministry priority. This priority emphasizes a ministry that reaches out to inactive members. Thus, this inactive member ministry was born.

The Lay Advisory Committee was recruited and helped with ministry development and implementation. They also recruited twenty-eight volunteers for the four weekly teams.

After the training phase, the teams conducted formal and informal visits. The volunteers participated in directed interviews immediately after the formal visits. Within one week after the formal visits, the inactive members were interviewed. At the end of the test period, the volunteers and inactive members contributed to an assessment of this ministry through follow-up, directed interviews.

After the ministry was developed, forty-eight local inactive members were identified. Twenty-four of them opted out and five had moved out of the local area. These actions resulted in a project population of nineteen inactive members who were afforded opportunities to share their stories. Fifteen inactive members provided reasons for their inactivity. Four inactive members returned to active church participation.

We now examine this ministry through the lenses of the learning goals and hypotheses to determine its overall effectiveness.

Evaluation of Learning Goals

The evaluation of the learning goals is derived from post-visit directed interviews and post-test period assessments. Each learning goal will be examined separately. The primary learning goal will be addressed first followed by the secondary learning goals.

Was a caring ministry consisting of prayer, telephone contacts, letters, and visits effective in rebuilding relationships with inactive members at LUMC? Based on the research, the project was successful in building some authentic personal relationships. It was revealed that not all parts of the ministry were equally effective in building relationships; however they all contributed to cultivating the environment in which personal relationships could be built.

As a participant-observer, I observed all aspects of this ministry. I classify the success level of this project as partial because of the mixed results found in the evaluation of the learning goals and hypotheses.

How effective was prayer in rebuilding relationships with inactive members at LUMC? The volunteers were asked to pray daily for the ministry and the inactive members throughout the test period.

The volunteers stated that the training sessions helped them to see the importance of prayer for the entire ministry. A few volunteers reported that the training provided some suggestions on how to pray for the ministry, themselves, and the inactive members. The debriefing interviews revealed that some volunteers relied on these suggestions each time they prayed. Several volunteers reported that prayer helped to remind them of the negative perceptions many active members have about inactive members. Some confessed that prayer was answered by God when their perceptions changed to seeing inactive members as God's beloved children and by calming their fears of receiving a negative reception by the inactive members. Others said that God helped them to remain focused on the intent of the ministry to build relationships with fellow church members.

Unfortunately, some team members reported that they prayed only just prior to making the visits. Others said that they prayed "every once in a while." Still others confessed that they had not prayed at all.

Prayer had an effect on the inactive members too. These effects were noted during the assessment interviews when the inactive members were informed that volunteers were praying for them. Most of them expressed surprise while others exhibited embarrassment. Following this revelation, several inactive members further reflected on their views of active church members and their reasons for not being active in the church.

Although not directly responsible for building relationships, I believe that prayer was important in enhancing the relationship-building process.

How effective were letters in rebuilding relationships with inactive members at LUMC? The only people who could inform us about the effects of the introductory letters were the inactive members. We received no positive responses to the letters via the response cards. Most interviewed inactive members reported that the letters informed them of the new ministry. Thirteen of the nineteen inactive members revealed that they had little expectation that the church would literally implement this ministry due to previous failed endeavors.

The letters informed the inactive members of the church's desire to relate to them. Therefore the letters served as a tool for providing the environment whereby relationships could be formed.

How effective were telephone calls in rebuilding relationships with inactive members at LUMC? The telephone call was another tool by which the church extended an invitation to inactive members to join this ministry. In the form of appointment-making and casual conversation, the inactive member could experience the volunteers' desire to connect with them on a personal level.

All of the volunteers and inactive members stated that the telephone calls did not directly build relationships. The calls served as the conduit to arrange the first formal visit between volunteers and inactive members.

Therefore the calls enabled relationship building but were not fully responsible for it.

How effective were formal face-to-face visits in rebuilding relationships with inactive members at LUMC? A number of relationships were reportedly built during these formal visits. Some turned out to be significant enough for a few inactive members to return to active church participation.

The volunteers reported that they believed they had built meaningful personal relationships with nine of the nineteen inactive members or 47.4 percent of inactive members within the reduced target population. Twelve inactive members, or 63.2 percent, reported that authentic personal relationships were built with them.

These formal contacts enabled the active and inactive members to begin the relationship-building process as a springboard to the informal opportunities. They were instrumental in setting up the informal contacts as the linchpin for more relationships to be formed. One inactive member commented that the formal visit served as the "ice breaker."

I sense that these formal visits were powerful because they helped the volunteers share, in a practical manner, the love of God. The interviews revealed no negative perceptions to the formal visits. As such, it appears that God's presence helped some volunteers and inactive members change their behaviors and attitudes about each other. This was evidenced by the inactive members who returned to active participation and by the volunteers who desired to expand this ministry to reach more than just inactive members.

How effective were informal contacts in rebuilding relationships with inactive members at LUMC? The informal contacts helped to increase the total number of relationships built. The volunteers believed that these visits helped to build and/or improve relationships with eleven inactive members, or 57.9 percent of the target group. Fourteen inactive members, or 73.7 percent, believed relationships had been built with them because of these chance contacts. These informal opportunities enhanced the relationship-building process. The increases over the formal visits' results show that a combination of formal and informal visits is needed to effectively build relationships with inactive members. The combination of formal and informal contacts provided the means by which volunteers and inactive members could remain relationally connected.

Evaluation of Hypotheses

We need to evaluate our hypotheses to provide an adequate understanding of this ministry. This evaluation will help in improving this ministry. There were five hypotheses for this ministry implementation.

Were all of the learning goals achieved? As stated above, all aspects of the ministry did not directly contribute to building relationships. The formal and informal visits were directly responsible for building and/or improving some relationships. The other meaningful parts of the ministry helped to prepare and facilitate these visits. The answer to this question is mixed.

Did some inactive members return to active church participation? I believed that some would return to the church because of the ministry, but my expectation was very low. I expected that only one or two people would return to active participation. During the test period, four inactive members returned to active church participation. Three began to attend Sunday worship on a regular basis. One person was participating in the midweek Bible study. This result was higher than I expected.

I am disappointed that the project did not result in more inactive members returning to active participation. I realized that some had been emotionally hurt so badly that they, without relying on God's power, would not choose to return. I can only pray that continued work and care with them will encourage them to lay aside their negative perceptions allowing them to reenter the church as active participants.

Did we rebuild positive relationships with 10 percent of the inactive members? The assessment of the learning goals showed we were able to build relationships with more than 10 percent of the participating inactive members. However, the directed interviews did not assess the quality of the relationships built.

We could assume that the reported relationships built were positive. If we accept this assumption, then positive relationships were built with more than 10 percent of the inactive members. However, this hypothesis could not be answered within the bounds of this ministry's test period. To evaluate this question, the directed interviews would have to delve deeper into the mind of the volunteers and inactive members with questions that evoke responses on their viewpoints of what makes a positive relationship.

Did 50 percent of the inactive members opt out of the ministry? Our implementation showed that 57.8 percent of the original identified forty-five local inactive members chose not to have any further contact with this inactive member ministry. This hypothesis was fairly accurate, but disappointing because of our inability to relate to these people.

This high ratio disturbed me deeply. The refusal to accept the invitation to connect relationally shows me that the spiritual interest may be low in many of our inactive members. It also showed me that we should not allow them to opt out of this ministry because of the person's lack of knowledge about the benefits for them and the church.

Did less than 10 percent of the active members volunteer for the caring ministry? When the recruitment phase of this ministry began, LUMC had 134 active church members. We recruited twenty-eight people, or 17.9 percent of the active membership, by the end of the recruitment phase. When the ministry was being implemented, the number of volunteers decreased to eighteen people or 13.4 percent of the active membership.

Although higher than the hypothesis, this low number of volunteers directly influenced the potential outcome by delaying the formal contacts with several inactive members. What is worse than the delay is that many active members did not accept the invitation to be in service to those in need.

Based on the evaluation of the learning goals and hypotheses, we can say that the ministry was partially successful. Furthermore, this evaluation revealed several ways in which this ministry could be improved.

What Would I Do Differently?

The analysis of the learning goals and hypotheses identified seven areas needing improvements. These areas are project leadership, the Lay

Advisory Committee, volunteer recruitment, volunteer training, inactive member selection process, ministry implementation, and evaluations.

Ministry Leadership

The leadership responsibilities were based on shared leadership roles between the pastor and a Lay Advisory Committee. As the pastor, I assumed many of the leadership tasks in this new ministry. I conducted every training session and attended every service night during ministry implementation. The Lay Advisory Committee had few leadership tasks to perform revolving around ministry development and evaluation. I recommend that the Lay Advisory Committee, without the pastor, serve as the ministry's leadership team. This would enable the pastor to oversee the ministry and provide objective pastoral guidance. Such a change may also help the laity to have a higher degree of ownership of this ministry.

I feel that this recommendation would also help the church's lay leadership to invest itself into the service ministries of its church. As they invest themselves into the implementation of this ministry, they can participate in God's redemptive actions through the acts of mercy extended to inactive members.

Referring to the design of the Methodist Societies, the implementation of this recommendation would help involve more people in small groups whereby spiritual growth may be experienced. As the ministry leadership team, these particular volunteers would have the opportunity to engage in at least two small groups associated with this ministry: the weekly teams and the Lay Advisory Group.

Within the UMC clergy appointment system, the average tenure for pastors at LUMC is 3.4 years. Therefore this particular modification may help the ministry survive the periodic pastoral changes. This would also help the ministry to be driven by the needs of the laity and not the personality or character of the appointed pastor.

Lay Advisory Committee

In conjunction with the above recommendation, I also recommend that the Lay Advisory Committee be expanded from three to eight people. This would equip each weekly team with two ministry leaders. This increased size will decrease the likelihood of ministry leadership not being available during ministry implementation and execution.

Volunteer Recruitment

I recommend that the length of time be extended from four weeks to eight weeks. This increased time could be combined with a more comprehensive recruitment program using more lay people. These lay people would be fully trained to conduct the small-group presentations and enrollment procedures. This increased time could allow the pastor to develop a sermon series around holiness, church membership, and the body of Christ. These sermons may enhance the recruitment process because of the encouragement from the congregation's clerical leader.

Volunteer Training

I recommend increasing the total training time to six hours consisting of three two-hour sessions. This increased training time would allow more time for the foundational theological discussions and more practical role-playing.

There were limited theological discussions during the training phase. The theological edification of the volunteers might help them to understand the importance of holiness with regard to this ministry. I also feel that this training might help some of them to understand God's high calling of Christians to actively participate within the priesthood of all believers. This training expansion might guide some volunteers to reflect on their relationship with God. It may help the volunteers to see how their divine-human relationship influences the effectiveness of this ministry.

The volunteers were generally ready for ministry, but most stated that more role-playing would improve their communication skills and decrease their anxieties. This expansion could incorporate spiritual aspects in order to help the volunteers talk more theologically with inactive members.

Inactive Member Selection Process

This ministry resulted in more than half of the local inactive members choosing not to participate. Therefore this ministry did not encompass all of the available local inactive members. I recommend that the inactive member selection process be slightly modified. The introductory letters need to be sent to the inactive members to prepare them for the new ministry. However, a response card does not need to be included with the letter because it made it too easy for inactive members to cut themselves off from this ministry.

My recommendation includes a way for inactive members to opt out of this ministry. When the visitation groups call the inactive members to coordinate the formal visits, the visitation groups could be given authority to *opt out* inactive members who are extremely adamant about not being visited. However, this option should be minimally used since inactive members do not fully understand the intent or possible benefits of the ministry. This option can also be exercised during the formal visits and subsequent directed interviews when an inactive member is perceived to be less than desirable to continue in the ministry.

Ministry Implementation

Ministry implementation went almost according to design. The refusal of one weekly team to implement the ministry could not be foreseen. There was no indication this would occur during the training phase. I recommend a signed covenant statement by the volunteers to express the importance of their commitment to the ministry. This may not have prevented what occurred during our implementation, but it would place individual accountability into the conduct of this ministry. The volunteers could express their commitment to God's redemptive work with this covenant. It would also impress upon the volunteers that the high calling of holiness requires us to respond to God's presence in ways that will please God.

The target group of this ministry needs to be expanded whereby the church can catch short-term inactive members before they become long-term inactive members. Our research showed that negative attitudes and behavioral changes occur between six to eight weeks after an event. Therefore worship absences must be tracked. This tracking is easily accomplished with most church membership software packages. Beginning with the third consecutive absence, the church member is placed on the inactive member roll. This placement would trigger the weekly team to contact them via a hand-written postcard extending our concern about their absence.

If a member continues to be absent for six consecutive weeks, then the weekly team, which would be a different team from three weeks prior, would make a telephone call with the inactive person to express more concern. This call would enable the inactive person to talk about what is causing his or her absence and to discuss possible solutions other than church absence.

If the continued absences extend to nine weeks, then the weekly team would conduct a visit with the inactive member to encourage him or her to return and to express the church's need for the member to return. If absences continue to twelve weeks, then the pastor is asked to make a pastoral visit to discuss membership vows and issues surrounding the absences.

Expansion of this ministry can also be with first-time and regular visitors. The teams can make a short visit with first-time visitors to show their appreciation for them attending the worship service. With this visit, the teams could provide a small thoughtful gift as an appreciation gift.

The visit with regular members would be to encourage them to become church members. The team members would need to be able to discuss church membership and the expectations of church members within the particular church. If this visit is successful in the regular visitor desiring to become a church member, then the ministry leadership would inform the pastor. The pastor would be expected to contact the regular visitor to arrange a pastoral discussion on church membership and when to join the church.

This ministry can also be expanded to include a writing component whereby the church could contact everyone connected to the church. This writing component could include thank you cards to first-time visitors, sympathy cards to grieving members, prayer cards to those on the prayer list, absences postcards to short-term inactives, thinking-of-you-cards to those in long-term nursing facilities, and cards to celebrate birthdays, anniversaries, and births. Of course, the list goes on to what you can contact people about.

There are other ways and people who you can include in this ministry. You literally can show that your church cares for everyone through the cards, calls, visits, and prayers. Only your imagination and willingness limit you in this ministry.

Evaluation

In the area of evaluation, the directed interviews worked well. However the pastor conducted the majority of the interviews. This may have prevented the inactive members from being fully forthcoming about their perceptions of the letter, prayers, calls, and visits. I recommend that the expanded Lay Advisory Committee conduct all directed interviews with the volunteers and inactive members. The Lay Advisory Committee could include the pastor in the evaluation interviews or conduct a periodic pastoral debriefing on the results.

Once again, I feel that this modification enables more lay people to be involved in this ministry whereby the opportunities to share God's love are increased. This modification may also enable a more forthcoming discussion between lay people whereby faith sharing and exhortation are more apt to be accomplished than was experienced during the pastor-lay person directed interviews.

Theological Reflection

This section reflects on what I have theologically struggled with throughout this ministry. It begins with a discussion on the helpfulness of Wesley's theology of holiness to this ministry. I follow this with my perceptions of inactive members. I conclude this section by reflecting on my personal journey. You could call this a time of confession by a pastor. I pray that it will help you—either a pastor or a layperson—endure the struggles of new ministry implementation.

The Helpfulness of Wesley's Theology

I gained a deeper understanding of Wesley's holiness theology. Wesley's theology was helpful to this ministry in the areas of God's presence, small groups, and personal relationships. His theology was also helpful in gaining an understanding of the deeper meaning of church membership.

Wesley's theology impressed upon me the importance of God's presence whereby God's power could be manifested among us. I was able to see this divine power demonstrated in several ways among the participants. It was best exemplified when God prompted people to volunteer to serve in this ministry. These people had no idea what the ministry would fully involve, yet they were willing to be used by God to pursue a congregational purpose.

Wesley's theology helped me to understand the effects of holiness with regard to love of neighbor. The love of God was transformed into love of neighbor in the conversations between the volunteers and inactive members. The influence of this divine love was reported as changed attitudes about inactive members by volunteers and changed behaviors of active church participation by some inactive members.

Wesleyan theology directed me toward seeing the connection of personal relationships to the redemptive actions of God. God's redemption resides within the divine-human relationship where it can be extended by believers through sharing God's love in their personal relationships. This personal connection between people cannot stop redemption because God is the One who grants it. However I believe that these relationships can enhance or hinder one's spiritual growth in response to God's actions.

Understanding the connection between God's love and serving others was aided by Wesley's theology. The love of God experienced by the volunteers was extended to the inactive members. I realized that the project provided multiple opportunities for God's love to be shared among people. From the Church Health Action Plan to the visits to the final assessments, these expressions of God's love helped us to serve God and each other. My hope is that the participants were encouraged to continue their pursuit of God's will in their lives after the project's completion.

The last area of helpfulness was in the area of small groups. Wesley's design of the Methodist Societies influenced the design of the weekly team meetings. The hope was that the volunteers would spiritually grow as they shared their experiences and perspectives. These reflections may have helped some people to see how God was working in, through, and for all of them.

Wesley's theology, though helpful in many ways, was not helpful in other ways. These ways included oversimplification of holiness, inability to meet expectations, and stringent accountability.

The first unhelpful area was the possible oversimplification of Wesley's theology. I rediscovered that Wesley's theology of holiness contains complex, redundant, and confusing terminology. Therefore some people may find it convenient to reduce this theology to a focus on the practical works of piety and mercy. One danger of this reductionist view is a spiritual checklist that promotes works' righteousness. This was seen during the project when one volunteer commented that his visitation group "checked the block." I expected spiritual transformation to occur in all participants but not as an event to be marked as complete. This reductionist perspective reduces God's role and elevates the human response. Thus real spiritual growth does not occur.

The second area that was not helpful was Wesley's expectations of church members. These expectations seem difficult to meet in our contemporary times. With many competing interests that Wesley did not have to deal with, some church members may slip into self-centeredness that may lead to breaking their membership vow instead of seeking ways to meet these membership expectations.

Wesley expected strict accountability among the Methodist Societies members as they pursued holiness. My observations revealed that strict accountability is not desired among most current Methodists. Therefore this may lead to refusal to participate in small groups where accountability is a key agenda item.

Wesley expected believers to pursue entire sanctification or Christian perfection. I disagree with Wesley that a perfected state of holiness is possible. In our world today, our perception of this perfect holiness causes me to disagree. Many believers may come very close, but I do not believe that Christians can maintain a perfected state of holiness. My concern is that a continued mantra on perfection may cause some people to abandon their holiness pursuit because of potential failure. This becomes another reason why people run through the church's revolving door.

Church Member Expectations

The UMC membership vow calls for a member "to be loyal to Christ through the United Methodist Church with their prayers, presence, gifts, service, and witness" (UMC *Discipline,* 143). However, it is apparent that many church members do not take these expectations seriously or they do not understand how they are to fulfill these expectations.

I discovered that some dimensions of holiness as Wesley proposed could be exhibited when members used these five areas to help guide their actions. However, less than 50 percent of our church members attend church on a regular basis and less than 25 percent participate in hands-on ministry service. Therefore the fulfillment of the membership expectations is severely lacking. I propose some instructional corrections on the membership expectations.

Prayer serves as the spiritual umbrella under which all other Christian actions are to be conducted. Prayer provides one of the means for God to communicate with believers. Lessons would discuss the influence that prayer has on spiritual growth and how actually to pray. Afterward, lay people ought to be given the opportunity to practice what they have learned about private and public prayers.

Presence suggests that members are to be present when the faith community comes together as the body of Christ. Lessons on this area would include a focus on the importance of the sacraments, worship, Christian education, fellowship, and accountability. When people are absent for an extended period of time, the church members need to extend their love of neighbor to the absentee members by contacting them in the effort to express care and concern.

Gifts are usually interpreted in financial terms. My expanded lessons on gifts would include spiritual gifts, time, talents, and other resources. Members would be encouraged to discover their spiritual gifts. As part of this discovery, they would discern how God is directing them to use those gifts in the edification of the church.

The first three areas may guide members toward Christian service. We learned that Wesley believed that all Christians should serve out of obedience and devotion to God. Lessons on service would be expanded to invite and encourage people to develop, implement, and modify ministries that aid in the spiritual growth of all people.

Witness is the faith story that is shared with others. By fulfilling the vow in the other four areas, members are provided the opportunity to share their faith stories. Instruction pertaining to witness would include why relationships with God and others are important to the individual's spiritual growth.

My Perceptions of Inactive Members

This ministry helped to change my perspective of inactive members. Although I have a changed perspective, I still have some concerns about inactive members.

As the ministry progressed, I was asked by a volunteer how I viewed inactive members. This question and subsequent personal reflection revealed that I was guilty of possessing and using the same negative terms that Knutson discussed. Therefore I was compelled to change my perception of inactive members so that I could better lead the church toward reaching out to inactive members.

My view of inactive members evolved toward seeing them as wayward sheep as portrayed in Luke 15. Individuals start out with good intentions when they become Christians and church members. However some members encounter things that cause them to wander away from the flock.

In Luke 15, the shepherd leaves the ninety-nine faithful sheep to track the one lost sheep. Upon finding the sheep, the shepherd caringly returns it to the flock. This ministry taught me that the church has a spiritual obligation to track and return wayward church members to the fellowship of the local church.

I realize that church members can decide for themselves not to return to active participation, but I learned that some might have legitimate reasons for their inactivity, such as employment. Therefore I ought to take into account the full range of reasons for inactivity instead of thinking negatively about inactive members.

This new perspective enables me to have empathy for the inactive members and to work toward ministries that reach out to them and ways to help them continue their spiritual growth outside the bounds of the church. I can endeavor to teach others to understand the complex realities of inactive members with the hope that people will implement an inactive member ministry.

I still have some concerns about inactive members, which are self-focus, lack of fellowship with the faith community, and lack of spiritual growth.

During the directed interviews, it appeared to me that several inactive members exhibited self-focus instead of God-focus. This revelation was found in the repeated explanation of why they could not attend Sunday worship. Not once did any of the inactives talk about how they can attend worship. There was no allusion to finding ways to participate in the life of the church outside any worship services.

This self-centered focus leads many inactive members not to participate in the available fellowship opportunities. Without this contact, inactive members have less chance of being equipped for ministry, being deployed for ministry, or being built up for future situations. Continued spiritual transformation is less likely to occur without the fellowship of other believers within the faith community.

My perception expresses my fear for the lack of spiritual growth in our inactive members. I avoided this discussion during the ministry test period. According to Wesley's teachings, inactive members are in spiritual danger because of their unproductive posture and their not following Christ in holiness.

If we use the membership vow as the means to observe the fruit of one's spiritual life, then it is quite possible to see little to no fruit produced by inactive members. I do not go as far as Wesley by saying that these people have lost their salvation, but there is some doubt as to their inward trust of God. It does show that these inactives do not endeavor to continue pursuing a Christ-like life.

I understand that spiritual growth is a personal matter, but the local church loses the use of inactive members' spiritual gifts. This loss means that the church cannot be as effective in achieving God's will as it could be with all members actively participating.

This fear for the spiritual welfare of inactive members and the influence on the church was present in me throughout this ministry. Although none of the inactive members reported a faith issue within themselves, I am still very concerned about their souls.

Personal Journey

I planned for a ministry that used relationships to draw people back to the local church. However, at the end of the ministry test period, I realized that relationships became the means to help people strive toward holiness. This end product was also seen in my spiritual journey.

The holiness theology informed me that my spirituality is still a work in progress because I have not reached Christian perfection. God uses my experiences to teach me about God's self and how I can relate to God better. Although I believe that Christian perfection is unlikely, this possibility still remains my goal and hope in this present life.

This project demonstrated to me that personal relationships are important. I have heard for many years that most people come to church because someone asked them to come. As a Christian and a pastor, I need to cultivate personal relationships within my church so that I can continue to grow spiritually and reach out to help others to grow spiritually.

Summary

In the UMC, the pursuit of holiness is an important theological reality. Ministries, such as this one, may help in placing a higher degree of emphasis on holiness and may lead to people being more committed to fulfilling their response to God's grace through the church.

Future Implications

The future implications I envision may occur in churches and my pastoral ministry.

I hope to influence other churches, pastors, and laypeople in the areas of relationship building, lay empowerment, reducing inactivity, and ministry expansion.

I believe that this project provided the opportunity for volunteers and inactive members to begin the process of relationship building. My hope is that this relationship building will continue well after the project is completed. As the building continues, I pray that God's power will enable volunteers and inactive members to come together so both are edified though God's grace.

This project helped LUMC continue its work on lay empowerment. Lay empowerment may be helped with training in shared leadership roles, relationship building, and ministry analysis. This expansion would include a focus on holiness theology.

The local church could explore ways to reduce its number of inactive members. I would require potential members to attend and graduate from a membership class before joining the church. This class would include lessons on membership expectations, holiness, and spiritual growth opportunities.

I also believe inactivity can be reduced through small-group ministry. Although there are several programs designed to help churches do this, I advocate a return to the basic design of the Methodist Societies. Through these small groups, people may actively pursue holiness because of its benefits to their spiritual growth.

As noted earlier in this chapter, this ministry should be expanded to include first-time visitors, sick members, shut-in members, and potential church members. This would help expand relationship building to all church members and potential members.

I pray that this book has been helpful to you. I hope that your ministry and church will blossom because of the thoughts that this ministry has begun in you.

I have seen this ministry implemented in three churches. All were grateful for taking a risk in reaching out to inactive church members, visitors, and active church members. I hope that you will take this same kind of risk in your ministry!

These future implications can have far-reaching possibilities. I pray that we can bring people back to our churches so that the body of Christ can achieve what God intends for it to accomplish. I pray for your overwhelming success as you implement this caring ministry. I also hope that you share the lessons you learn as you implement this caring ministry.

As I conclude this book, allow me to use a quote from John Wesley, who reportedly said it on his deathbed. I know that you are not on your deathbed and I hope that your church is not either, but Wesley's quote will help to keep things in its proper perspective as you and I continue to do ministry that will help others become more like Christ. John Wesley's final words were, "Best of all, God is with us."

I thank God for your ministry and your willingness to pursue this kind of caring ministry in its expanded form. I thank God that the Holy Spirit is with all of us. It is time for you to get started with your caring ministry in your church! Together, with lots of hard work, we can stop the church's revolving door!

Works Cited

Balz, Horst ed. *Exegetical Dictionary of the New Testament.* PC Study Bible CD-ROM Version 5.0. Seattle: Biblesoft, Inc., 2007. CD-ROM.

Barnes, Albert. *Barnes' Notes on the New Testament.* PC Study Bible CD-ROM Version 5.0. Seattle: Biblesoft, Inc. 2007., CD-ROM.

Buttrick, George Arthur. *The Interpreter's Bible.* Vol. 10. New York: Abingdon Press, 1953. Print.

Calvin, John et al. *Commentary Notes for the Geneva Bible.* PC Study Bible CD-ROM Version 5.0. Seattle: Biblesoft, Inc., 2007. CD-ROM.

Clarke, Adam. *Clarke's Commentary.* PC Study Bible CD-ROM Version 5.0. Seattle: Biblesoft, Inc., 2007. CD-ROM.

Collins, Raymond F. *Sacra Pagina Series: Volume 7: First Corinthians.* Collegeville, Minnesota: The Liturgical Press, 1999. Print.

Coutsoumpos, P. *Community, Conflict, and the Eucharist in Roman Church.* Lanham, Maryland: University Press of America, 2006. Print.

Cross, Bryan R. "Apostolicity." http://www.geocities.com/metaphysics8/Apostolicity.html. Website.

Custer, Chester E. *The United Methodist Primer.* Nashville: Discipleship, 2001. Print.

Dudley, Carl S. *Effective Small Churches in the Twenty-first Century.* Nashville: Abingdon, 2003. Print.

Dunn, James D. G. *The Theology of Paul the Apostle.* Grand Rapids: William B. Eerdmans Publishing Company, 1998. Print.

Frank, Thomas Edward. *Polity, Practice, and the Mission of the United Methodist Church.* Nashville: Abingdon, 1997. Print.

Gray, L. Charles. *Reaching the Drop Out Church Member.* New York: United Presbyterian Church in the USA, 1982. Print.

Heitzenrater, Richard P. *Wesley and the People Called Methodists*. Nashville: Abingdon, 1995. Print.

Keener, Craig S. *The IVP Bible Background Commentary*. PC Study Bible CD-ROM Version 5.0. Seattle: Biblesoft, Inc., 2007. CD-ROM.

Knutson, Gerhard. *Ministry to Inactives*. Minneapolis: Augsburg, 1979. Print.

Langford, Thomas A. *Practical Divinity: Theology in the Wesleyan Tradition*. Nashville: Abingdon, 1983. Print.

Maddox, Randy L. *Responsible Grace: John Wesley's Practical Theology*. Nashville: Kingswood, 1994. Print.

"Maslow's Hierarchy of Needs." *Wikipedia: The Free Encyclopedia*. Wikimedia Foundation, 2001–2010. Web. 17 Dec. 2008. Website.

McGrath, Alister E. *Christian Theology: An Introduction*. Malden, Massachusetts: Blackwell, 1997. Print.

Miller, Herb. *Church Effectiveness Nuggets: Volume 6: How to Shrink Your Church's Inactive Member List*. http://www.theparishpaper.com/webfm_send/32. Website.

Outler, Albert C., and Richard P. Heitzenrater. *John Wesley's Sermons*. Nashville: Abingdon, 1991. Print.

Runyon, Theodore. *The New Creation: John Wesley's Theology Today*. Nashville: Abingdon, 1998. Print.

Savage, Carl, and William Presnell. *Narrative Research in Ministry*. Louisville: Oates, 2008. Print.

Savage, John S. *The Apathetic and Bored Church Member*. Pittsford, New York: LEAD, 1976. Print.

Savage, John S. *Listening and Caring Skills in Ministry*. Nashville: Abingdon, 1996. Print.

Stokes, Mack B. *Major United Methodist Beliefs*. Nashville: Abingdon, 1989. Print.

The United Methodist Church. *The Book of Discipline of the United Methodist Church 2008*. Nashville: Abingdon, 2009. Print.

The United Methodist Church. *The United Methodist Book of Worship*. Nashville: Abingdon, 1992. Print.

Walvoord, John F. ed. *Bible Knowledge Commentary*. PC Study Bible CD-ROM Version 5.0. Seattle: Biblesoft, Inc., 2007. CD-ROM.

Wesley, John. *Explanatory Notes upon the New Testament.* Grand Rapids: Baker, 1983. Print.

---. *Journal of John Wesley.* Ed. Percy Livingstone Parker. *PC Study Bible.* Comp. James G. Gilbertson. Ver. 5.0. Seattle: Biblesoft, 2007. CD-ROM.

---. *Sermons of John Wesley.* 1771 and 1872 eds. 4 vols. *PC Study Bible.* Comp. James G. Gilbertson. Ver. 5.0. Seattle: Biblesoft Inc., 2007. CD-ROM.

---. *The Works of John Wesley.* 3rd ed. 14 vols. Grand Rapids: Baker, 1978. Print.

Wiersbe, Warren W. *The Bible Exposition Commentary.* PC Study Bible CD-ROM Version 5.0. Seattle: Biblesoft, Inc., 2007. CD-ROM.

Appendices

Appendix A: Contemporary Wesleyan Theologians

Appendix B: Ministry Organizational Structure

Appendix C: Volunteer Enrollment Form

Appendix D: Weekly Bulletin Appeals

Appendix E: Group Enrollment Presentation

Appendix F: Pulpit Announcements

Appendix G: Team Member Training Handbook

Appendix H: Listening Skills Forms

Appendix I: Training Sessions

Appendix J: Role-Playing Scenarios

Appendix K: Introductory Letter

Appendix L: Response Card

Appendix M: Visitation Report Forms

Appendix A

Contemporary Wesleyan Theologians

Wesley's holiness theology has been modified slightly since his proclamations on it. However the pursuit of Wesley's holiness has changed in contemporary times. Several authors provide us a contemporary view of Wesley's holiness theology.

Alister McGrath wrote an introductory Christian theology textbook in which he described Wesley's desire as "the need for a living faith," thus the "experiential side of Christian faith" (McGrath, 81). The experience of God's grace within the lives of believers prompted the Wesley and the Methodist movement. McGrath believed that Wesley holiness theology made "Christianity relevant and accessible to the experiential situation of the masses" (McGrath 91). To maintain relevancy, believers must continue their pursuit of holiness. Wesley's pursuit of holiness in his own life helped him to maintain relevancy with those in the Methodist movement as they strove for holy living. Several authors noted that this relevancy comes from Wesley's focus on spiritual transformation enabled by God.

Richard Heitzenrater believes that Wesley's theological focus was on people achieving a "practical holiness" (Heitzenrater, 30). Holiness is a spiritual transformation "of heart and life" (Heitzenrater, 30). The transformation continues as Christians matures until they have "the mind of Christ and walk as He walked" (Heitzenrater, 307).

In order for people to have the mind of Christ, people need God to work actively in their lives. This divine work enables them to respond to God. Randy Maddox wrote that Wesley's theology relies exclusively on God's grace. God's grace empowers people to become Christians by having faith in God. Maddox believed that the Christian life is a constant transformation of sanctification brought about by God's grace. "Such transformation is realized by our subsequent responsible participation in

God's sanctifying grace" (Maddox, 177). Holiness as a human response to God's grace guides believers toward being more like Christ.

Wesley's theology points toward "the importance of holiness in our actions" (Maddox, 178). Holiness in our outward actions manifests the inward spiritual transformation. This transformation empowers Christians to love God and neighbor. Albert Outler and Richard Heitzenrater write that the unbeliever is radically transformed so that his/her desires turn from the world "unto God" (Maddox, 65). This continuous change is further demonstrated in sanctification as one bears the "necessary fruit of love of neighbor" (Maddox, 179). Outler and Heitzenrater imply that Wesley's theology places an importance on personal relationships.

These personal relationships begin with God. As this divine-human relationship deepens, the believer is encouraged to enter into personal relationships with his or her neighbor as a response to the love he or she experienced in the divine-human relationship. How are these personal relationships to God and neighbor manifested within the church?

Wesley's teachings on the means of God's grace "is confirmed in the [current] evangelical experience" (Langford, 21). Wesley's holiness theology is further reflected in "existentialist themes, reaffirmation of traditional doctrines, black liberation theology, and process philosophy" (Langford, 225). The holiness theology of Wesley has a contemporary following outside the denominations with a Wesleyan heritage.

Two Wesleyan scholars help us examine the role of the local church in helping church members move toward holiness. Alister McGrath believes that holiness enables the believer to have "a living faith" (McGrath, 81). Believers show evidence of this living faith when they serve others through the church's ministries. Thomas Langford believes that the role of the local church is to provide a ministry structure that enables believers to pursue "God's will and activity" (Langford, 226). As to how the church structures itself to allow this pursuit is left to individual interpretation and ministry implementation. The local church is to organize itself by focusing on "the lay practice of piety and mercy in everyday life, as well as lay leadership in education, social reform, and mission" (Langford, 143).

McGrath and Langford imply that love of God and neighbor, as guided by God's grace, enables church members to care for others inside and outside the church. Thomas infers that this care is to occur through the church's ministries. Therefore the church's ministries may help to establish and to improve personal relationships between believers and those being served.

Theodore Runyon believes that "Wesley understood God's goal as the transformation of this present age, restoring health and holiness to God's creation" (Runyon, 169). He sees that this goal is achieved when "all things are restored to [God's] intended state" (Runyon, 169). The pursuit of holiness by individuals within society can be seen when church members take seriously their responsibility to care for each other. Runyon implies that this can be seen in the pursuit of social justice within the world among the various issues that present themselves among us. He implies that church members are to be "in participation with God's redemptive enterprise [as] faith working by love bringing holiness and happiness to all the earth." This occurs today "when we confront the injustices of the present age" (Runyon, 170).

The writers tend to agree with Wesley's theology as Wesley designed. However their contemporary viewpoints show that this theology of holiness has evolved to confront current issues. The theology of holiness is capable of being interpreted across a wide array of stances from liberal to conservative extremes.

These contemporary theologians see that Wesley is relevant in today's age. This relevancy is seen as the theology of holiness is applied to different issues and in varying manners. However they seem to point out that active participation within the local church is necessary for Christians to participate in the redemption efforts of God. These redemption efforts have the objective of spiritually transforming humanity so that it can aid in the transformation of the world.

Appendix B

Ministry Organizational Structure

This structure was used within a local United Methodist church. However this structure will work in any church.

This new ministry was established initially as an ad hoc ministry for the test period. If the ministry were to be continued, it would come under the umbrella of the Nurture Ministries Area, which is responsible for ministries that mainly focus on the church membership and those who relate to the church with their participation.

The leadership for this ministry consists of the Lay Advisory Committee (LAC) and the senior pastor. When the continuation occurs, the senior pastor would be removed and the LAC would serve as the ministry's lay leadership. The LAC consists of four laypeople. One LAC member would serve on each weekly team.

There are four weekly teams, which are named on the acronym of CARE. Within each team, there are a team captain and subteams. The subteams are arranged according to the work areas. Therefore the subteams would be called the praying team, the writing team, the calling team, the visiting teams, and the child-CARE team. Ideally there would be two people in each of the subteams, except for the visiting teams. The intent of this ministry is to make face-to-face contact whereby relationships can be reestablished or nurtured. Therefore most of the people on the weekly teams would be focused on visiting. You can have as few as ten people on the various subteams. However, more people who volunteer for the ministry enables you to have more visitation teams.

You can modify this structure where you have people conducting the administrative tasks that are associated with this ministry, such as attendance tracking, team meeting preparations of the assignment sheets, and follow-up actions.

Appendix C

Volunteer Enrollment Form

This form was used to enroll volunteers into the caring ministry.

Caring Ministry
Become a Caregiver Today!

ENROLLMENT FORM

I want to commit to serve as a Caregiver!

NAME:_____

ADDRESS:_____

CITY, STATE, ZIP:_____

TELEPHONE: _____

E-MAIL:_____

I want to serve on (circle one):

C Team (1ˢᵗ Tuesday)   A Team (2ⁿᵈ Tuesday)

R Team (3ʳᵈ Tuesday)   E Team (4ᵗʰ Tuesday)

I am most interested in doing (circle two):

Visiting   Praying

Calling   Writing

Child Care   Hospitality

Appendix D
Weekly Bulletin Appeals

These appeals appeared in the four weekly bulletins during the volunteer recruitment phase. These appeals could be used in the expanded recruitment period.

Week 1

Do You Care?

Our congregation saw a need to show we care for our members. A new caring ministry is being established to show that we care. If you can pray, write, talk, or visit, then you are needed for this new ministry. You only volunteer for one Tuesday night a month for two hours. You can enroll today! At the end of the service, visit the enrollment table and become a caregiver!

Week 2

We Choose to Care

A church in Colorado has the motto "We Choose to Care." It shows that the church made some choices to become involved and concerned with the needs of others. Our church chooses to be a church that cares when sorrow, sickness, and loneliness come. We have a new ministry that shows that we care. This ministry has room for more servants. This new ministry reaches out to people within our church. This ministry enables you to care for people by relating to them in a caring way. All you have to do is to enroll on the Tuesday night that fits your schedule. All we ask you to do is to commit to care one night each month for two hours. We look forward to you being a vital part of this new ministry. At the end of the service, visit the enrollment table and become a caregiver!

Week 3

Do You Care?

Everyone can care for two hours per month! That is right—only two hours on one Tuesday night per month! A new caring ministry is looking for people to pray, call, write, and visit church members and visitors. This ministry takes place on Tuesdays between 6:30 and 8:30 p.m. Why not take the step to show that our church and you care? Enroll in one of our teams after the worship service today at the enrollment table! Become a caregiver!

Week 4

New Caring Ministry Begins Soon!

The caring ministry is filling up fast with compassionate volunteers! However there is still room for you! The small commitment is two hours on one Tuesday night per month. Training will begin soon. Help our church show the love of God to others as we care in God's name as we reach out to others. Enroll right after the worship service today at the enrollment table! Become a caregiver!

Appendix E

Group Enrollment Presentation

This presentation was conducted with small groups, such as Sunday School classes, men's and women's groups, youth groups, and Bible study groups. At the end of the presentation, those present were able to complete an enrollment form (appendix C). The appearance of the slides is to be modified to fit your local church. You can modify the content and arrangement of the slides, but this is what worked well for us.

Slide 1

Caring Ministry

Becoming a Caregiver Today!

Note: Clip art and/or pictures are useful here to convey the kind of work areas that need to be filled.

Slide 2

Caring Ministry Is and Is Not

- Caring Ministry is an ongoing ministry that adapts to the gifts of people. Caring Ministry is not another program.
- Caring Ministry is mobilizing all church members. Caring Ministry is not a particular person's personality.
- Caring Ministry is supportive of the church's current ministries. Caring Ministry is not a substitute for other ministries.
- Caring Ministry is improving the church's health. Caring Ministry is not some other church's footprint on us.

Slide 3

The Great Commission

We used Matthew 28:19 as the scriptural passage that motivated us toward caring for other church members.

- We believe that the Great Commission means that each church member is to endeavor to take care of each other, which includes those who are inside and outside the body of Christ.
- We believe that the Great Commission means that church members are to actively care for others with the love of Christ flowing through them.
- We believe that the Great Commission means that church members must reach out to inactive church members, worship service visitors, and unchurched people.
- We believe that the Great Commission means that we are to use all of the means to our disposal to care for others with God's compassion.

Slide 4

The Body of Christ

We used 1 Corinthians 12:24–27 as the scriptural passage that reminds us about our responsibility to each other within the body of Christ.

- One body.
- Connect to each other if we recognize this connection or not.
- Called to care for those who are inside and outside the church.

Slide 5

The Areas of Ministry

- Pray: Prayers for the subteams and their work.
- Write: Letters and cards to those on the assignment sheets.

- Call: Telephone calls to arrange visit appointments and to check on others on the assignment sheets.
- Child care: Help children make cards to be sent to sick, shut-in, and missed church members.
- Visit: Visits to inactive church members and first-time visitors.

Note: This slide displays the various work areas of the caring ministry and what the results of the work are.

Slide 6

Caring Opportunities

Caring Ministry meets on Tuesdays at 6:30 p.m.

We need:
- Team captains: They will oversee the weekly activities, distribute the assignment sheets, assist in recruiting, resolve issues, and complete progress reports.
- Team members: They will serve once a month for two hours.

Caring Teams Meeting Days
C team – first Tuesday evening of the month
A team – second Tuesday evening of the month
R team – third Tuesday evening of the month
E team – fourth Tuesday evening of the month

Slide 7

Where He Leads Me

Note: This can be any hymn that conveys the commitment needed to perform this ministry. We used the verses and the refrain of Edward W. Blandy and John Samuel Norris's "Where He Leads Me." This hymn, which is under public domain, helped us to recognize that God has a place for all of us to serve with the gifts that God has blessed us with. The caring ministry was a great place to put those spiritual gifts to use.

Slide 8

Questions

Time to Enroll

Note: After the presentation was complete, we entertained any questions. After the questions were dispensed with, we asked those in attendance to enroll using the enrollment form.

Appendix F

Pulpit Announcements

These announcements were made during the primary worship services. At the end of each worship service, the lay speakers staffed the enrollment table where the active church members were given the opportunity to enroll. The first appeal is conducted by the pastor, but the enrollment table is manned by a lay person. The other announcements were accomplished by members of the Lay Advisory Committee.

First Week

"Do you care? We are implementing a new caring where we are asking you to commit to caring for two hours one night a month. We are not asking you to care for the whole month, just two hours each month. You can do that! That is right. Only two hours per a month. Can you write? Most of us can. Can you talk on the phone? Absolutely. Can you visit someone who is in need? Everyone can do one or more of these tasks. We need forty people to sign up. The ministry night is on Tuesdays and starts at 6:30 p.m. You can choose which Tuesday night fits best with your schedule. Two hours a month is a small amount of time to show that you care in the name of Christ. So today, will you take the step to show that the Lakeland Church and you care? The enrollment table will be in front of the church right after this worship service. If you have any questions, there will be someone there to answer them. I know that you care. Now is the time to show it! Thank you."

Second Week

"I am here to talk to you about our new caring ministry. We will focus on building relationships with inactive church members and visitors. We will enable our church members to tell their stories. We think they will be appreciative that we are thinking about them after being out of the church for so long. Our visitors will be able to tell us what they think about our church as we extend an invitation for them to worshipping with us. God can work through us in this new ministry. For this ministry to be successful, we need more people to sign up. Praying, calling, visiting, and writing are the tasks to be performed. Through these tasks, we will share the love of God with others. Please consider being a part of this new caring ministry by enrolling today at the enrollment table. I will be there to help you. Thank you."

Third Week

"Do you care? We asked this question for the last two weeks. I said, 'Yes, I want to care.' I signed up. Then my anxiety started going up. What have I done? What am I getting into? The pastor is there for you. He will be providing us with training for this ministry. The training book has examples for us to follow. The training plan includes communication skills, role-playing, perceptions, and visitation techniques. I pray that I will be a blessing to someone. One of the true blessings will be mine. I am a member of the R team. So, do you care? We are looking for people who want to serve God by caring for others. Praying, calling, writing, visiting, and caring are all you would have to do. You can do this! You too will be blessed! Please sign up today after this worship service at the enrollment table. Thank you!"

Fourth Week

"Hello. Being a member of one of our caring teams gives people the opportunity to minister to members of the body of Christ. This ministry does not require great strength, fierce courage, or vast knowledge. All it requires is a loving spirit, an open heart, and a desire to see the body of Christ in unity. It asks for a small sacrifice of time and energy. Yet this ministry can reach those parts of the body of Christ who need encouragement, consolation, prayer, or a kind word. We, who are able, should lift up those who are not. We need to let them know that the body is not whole without them. First Corinthians 12:25 states, 'God has combined the members of the body. It has given greater honor to the parts that lacked it so that there should be no division in the body. But, its parts should have equal care for each other.' Help us make our church stronger and healthier. Join us on Tuesday evenings for the caring ministry. You will bless many and will receive blessings yourself. Sign up after this worship service at the enrollment table. I will be there to answer any questions you may have about this ministry. I am looking forward to working with you all. Thank you."

Appendix G
Team Member Training Handbook

This handbook is given to each volunteer during the training phase. It details the training that occurred within the two sessions. It can be expanded to include other items that the Lay Advisory Committee deem important. It is written for a United Methodist congregation, but you can adapt it to your particular denomination and doctrine.

Caring Ministry

Becoming a Caregiver!

Sharing the Love of Christ!

Team Member Notebook

Our Desire to Care

Are you ready to care? Do you really want to care? Do we, as a church, really care?

The care ministry is the result of asking and answering these difficult questions. There are many thousands of unchurched people in our city. In most churches, ours included, less than 33 percent of its members actively participate. We seem to desire a way to serve our community and church while we are faithful to the Great Commission that Jesus gave us.

Our only desire is to see that we, as a church, understand the Great Commission and how we can use the God-given gifts to care for those around you. We want to see our church members actively reaching out to others.

This caring ministry is not a program but an ongoing ministry adapted to the gifts and needs of our church and community. This caring ministry is not a substitute or a replacement for any current ministries but supports all of the other church ministries. This caring ministry asks each church member to give God only two hours each month.

We want to see you as a servant of Christ sharing the love and care of God.

The pages that follow are tools and tips that will help you to effectively care.

Theological Background

Holiness is a dominating theme in John Wesley's theology. From Wesley's perspective, a person can be "holy of heart and holy in life." Before a person can pursue this holiness, he or she must have a relationship with God through Jesus Christ.

Holiness is God renewing the divine image within the believer. This action prompts a person's response to God's love with spiritual transformation made possible by God's grace. God loves us and we respond with love of God with all our heart, soul, mind, and strength. This love of God empowers believers to love their neighbors as themselves. The achievement of these loves is possible only by God's grace.

Such spiritual transformation can lead to authentic personal relationships. God's grace can help believers relate to each other in a nurturing manner. This nurturing manner can lead to a deeper level of trust that allows believers to help each other strive for holiness. This deeper trust among people can lead to healthy personal relationships.

Holiness provides the theological foundation for Methodist Christians. This foundation encourages us to live out our response to God's grace in good works that exemplify love of God and neighbor. This theology elevates nurture and care for others as the mission and service of Methodist Christians. This understanding is clearly expressed in the church member expectations found in the *Book of Discipline.*

In order to be members of the UMC, individuals take a membership vow to be loyal to Christ through the UMC "with their prayers, presence, gifts, service, and witness" (UMC *Book of Worship,* 109). These areas provide the structure to hold members accountable for living a Christian life of holiness. However, members do not take this vow to strive for a holy lifestyle in a vacuum. Each member in the local UMC congregation makes a vow to love, confirm, and strengthen the new member.

The absence of the inactive members causes the church to be in a weakened spiritual state by the loss of the inactive members' spiritual gifts. The church will not be as effective as it can be until the inactive members return and become active parts of the church. The church is charged to prepare all members for ministry in the world. This is not achievable when inactive members are not present to serve in these ministries.

The hope of the church's ministries is the edification of all members and those being served by the church's ministries. Absence from the church severely limits the achievement of this goal. When all inactive members return to active church participation, the church is able to use all of the available spiritual gifts in application to the church's ministries. Until this occurs, the active membership is called to reach out to the inactive members.

The Function Tasks of The Caring Ministry

The function of this caring ministry is found in the various components of Reach. These components ensure that we have a comprehensive and far-reaching ministry that impacts all people with any kind of relationship to LUMC. These components create a caring environment within our church in which to worship and serve God in the same manner in which Jesus cared for people during His earthly ministry.

Hand-Reach

This avenue is important and essential. It applies to you if you have the gift of administration, craftsmanship, and creativity. The tasks that seem tedious to most are tremendous opportunities for you to truly care for the church and community. The following assignments answer this question: what do I do to care?

Administrative assignments: The caring ministry will constantly spur interest in our church and people will request information. Part of the administrative assignment will be following up on getting the requested information into the hands of those interested in different aspects of how our church functions, as well as help the ministries of our church. This area also includes the processing of the worship attendance so that the other work areas are able to conduct their ministries. Caring is accomplished through your diligence in allowing staff members to focus on other areas of ministry without being inundated with administrative tasks for this caring ministry.

Attendance tracking: This assignment allows you to help track the attendance of visitors and members. This is used to generate cards, letters, calls, and visits within the caring ministry. This group meets on Monday mornings to note attendance, absences, prospects, and visitors. Care is accomplished through your focus on the importance of worship attendance and your love to see our church grow.

Promotion assignments: This assignment helps to recruit more people into the caring ministry. Promotional projects include posters, signs, manning the enrollment table, and announcements during the worship services. How effective we are in promoting this caring ministry will enable others to enjoy serving God by caring for others. Care is accomplished through your enthusiasm for others to serve God.

Heart-Reach

Hospitality is an exciting and necessary avenue of the caring ministry. This ministry eliminates some of the more common objections people have for not participating in this ministry. Hospitality is the springboard which frees other team members to exercise their gifts. The person who participates in the avenue of hospitality has just as much a part in the salvation of an evangelistic prospect as the person who actually led them to Christ. In fact, not having hospitality in our caring ministry will keep many people from having the opportunity to participate. The following assignments answer this question: what do I do to care?

> **Child care assignments (if necessary):** This assignment creates freedom for our weekly teams. As your hospitality provides child care for people, they, in turn, will be able to concentrate on their caring tasks and assignments. This area is for children who are younger than elementary school.

> **Children Caring:** This assignment entails working with elementary school-aged children to construct postcards and posters that will be sent to our shut-ins, sick, hospitalized, or those who are in need of encouragement. This would entail the supervision of children with the projects. Care is accomplished through your artisanship and special touch.

In-Reach

The first avenue of care is ministering and meeting needs within our church. We must not reach out to those outside of the church at the expense of our members. People need to know that a giant push is taking place to make a difference in our community, but *their* needs will not be sacrificed. This avenue will improve our church's health. In history, every great nation has fallen from within. We cannot allow this to happen to our church. The following assignments answer this question: what do I do to care?

Absentee assignments (work areas: call, visit, write): These assignments are given to care for people who have not attended a worship service for more than three weeks. The purpose is to find out if there is any problem that has kept them away from the fellowship of God's people and church. The intent of these assignments is to contact a person every few weeks until he or she returns into the fold of the church or begins active participation at another one of God's churches.

Elderly assignments (work areas: call, visit, write): These assignments are given to care for our senior church members who are physically unable to attend church. These people have served the church for many years and are now unable to actively serve. It is essential that they are made to feel included in our church and that they are still important to the life of the church. The calls and writings will occur on the regular ministry night. Visits will be coordinated so that they will occur during daylight hours at the conveniece of the caring team members. The activity will also involve the creation and writing of cards.

Encouragement assignments (work areas: call, write): These assignment are given to uplift members of our church and leaders within our community. They make people aware that what they are doing is important and impacting lives. The people included in this area include sick, shut-ins, recently hospitalized, grieving, church leaders, and community elected officials. Those who are ministered to can be expanded to include anyone who the Lay Advisory Committee deems in need of encouragement.

Commitment assignments (work areas: call, visit, write): These assignments are given to care for the people who are new members of our church. This is a chance to celebrate with them for their decision to join our faith community. This is a way for us to affirm their decision and follow up on potential questions that they may have. These assignments also include reaching out to regular visitors and inviting them to become full church members.

Outreach

One of our most important functions as a church body is to transport our care outside the walls of our worship center. Refer once again to the Great Commission found in Matthew 28:19. This avenue effectively covers a wide span of outreach needs. The following assignments will be given in this avenue and answer this question: what do I do to care?

Unchurched assignments (work areas: visit, call): These assignments are given to care for a larger population of the community. These assignments help open the door for God's work. These are people who we know for certain are in need of the good news of Jesus Christ. Whether they themselves have expressed the need or someone else has, these assignments have a high priority.

Community encouragement (work areas: write, call): These assignments are given to help affirm care by encouraging community leaders, school teachers, public safety officials, and others. These are requested through our prayer-request cards.

Prospect assignments (work areas: call, visit, write): These assignments focus on first-time visitors, regular visitors (visited more than four times in a three-month period), and inactive members. This assignment entails being able to cover a wide scope because of the potential discussions that can occur.

Up Reach

The next and most vital avenue of this caring ministry is prayer. Prayer is the grease that keeps this ministry moving in God's direction. Prayer helps us to stay plugged into our power source of God. Like a light, we cannot shine unless we stay plugged into our source for power. In the same sense, our caring ministry is dependent upon prayer. It is the difference between being a good ministry and a caring ministry. These assignments are conducted during the opening and celebration of each ministry night and during the regular course of the weekly meeting night.

> **Church prayer assignments (work area: pray):** This avenue deals with those needs within our church family. These needs are communicated through the prayer-request cards that we receive each week. As we pray for each other, the care and concern for one another will promote unity and fellowship.

> **Community prayer assignments (work area: pray):** This avenue deals with those needs expressed for people outside our church. These needs are communicated through contacts made through the various forms of outreach. Caring for our community begins with praying for our community. The greatest thing we can do for our community is stand in the gap on their behalf in prayer.

Viewpoints

Active and inactive church members have different viewpoints about themselves and about other church members. Gerhard Knutson's book *Ministry to Inactives* helps us to understand these perceptions so that we can come to grips with our viewpoints of inactive members and have some comprehension about what inactive members think of us.

Knutson writes that:

- Active members see inactive members as dropouts, delinquents, do-nothings, inactive, lazy, backsliders, sinners, complainers, and excuse makers.
- When dealing with inactive members, active members feel frustrated, fearful, anxious, worried, hostile, suspicious, full of pity, sympathetic, puzzled, and embarrassed.
- Inactive members view active members as hypocrites, do-gooders, nosy, fussy, nitpickers, bosses, the *in* group, judges, and high and mighty.
- When dealing with active members, inactive members feel condemned, forgotten, left out, lonely, rejected, abandoned, angry, suspicious, and like failures.

Gerhard Knutson writes, "Evangelism does not mean waiting for the 'inactive' to 'come to us' but rather it means that God's people, who know and experience and love the gospel, begin to examine their own attitudes. Our ministry to the 'inactives' begins by overcoming certain attitudes and names in order that the energy and love of the gospel may rightly and lovingly motivate us. If an 'inactive' person who may feel abandoned or rejected sees the 'active' person as a hypocrite or do-gooder, and then visited by someone who treats him as a drop out or delinquent, the results could be empty. Or they could be explosive! The gospel enables us, through grace and forgiveness, to accept people where they are and to begin genuinely to care about them. It enables us to come in a non-threatening, non-judgmental manner and thus to model the gospel as well as to speak the gospel."

John Savage, in *The Apathetic and Bored Church Member,* calls what the inactive member feels as the "Anxiety-Anger Complex." "Movement away from active church involvement is triggered by some kind of initial anxiety. Anxiety is a feeling of loss of a comfortable state. It is an awareness of discomfort. Anxiety may range from vague feelings of uneasiness, restlessness, and foreboding to specifically identified fears." At some point in the inactive member's life, this anxiety moves to anger. "Anger may be best described as a combination of uneasiness, discomfort, tenseness, resentment and frustration. Anger is the response to anxiety occurring when a person feels comfort is being taken away. Anger attempts to get rid of the objects or situations producing anxiety. Anger is a means of returning to a comfortable state."

This caring ministry is important as our church reconnects with inactive members. We work together to rebuild the relationships with all of our members, not just the active ones.

Active Listening Skills

This portion comes from John Savage's book titled *Listening and Caring Skills in Ministry*.

1. **Pay attention.** One goal of active listening is to set a comfortable tone and allow time and opportunity for the other person to think and speak. Pay attention to your frame of mind as well as your body language. Be focused on the moment and operate from a place of respect.

2. **Withhold judgment.** Active listening requires an open mind. As a listener and a leader, you need to be open to new ideas, new perspectives, and new possibilities. Even when good listeners have strong views, they suspend judgment, hold their criticism, and avoid arguing or selling their own viewpoints.

3. **Reflect.** Learn to mirror the other person's information and emotions by paraphrasing key points. Do not assume that you understand correctly or that the other person knows you have heard him or her. Reflecting is a way to indicate that you and your counterpart are on the same page.

4. **Clarify.** Do not be shy to ask questions about any issue that is ambiguous or unclear. Open-ended, clarifying, and probing questions are important tools. They draw people out and encourage them to expand their ideas while inviting reflection and thoughtful response. Positive use of questions includes garnering free information (information given to you without asking), filling in missing information to clarify ideas, or discovering the perspective of certain words that was used. This helps us conduct

a perception check with the inactive member. This helps connect to the speaker's feelings in a caring and sensitive manner.

5. **Summarize.** Restating key themes as the conversation proceeds confirms and solidifies your grasp of the other person's point of view. It also helps both parties to be clear on mutual responsibilities and follow-up. Briefly summarize what you have understood as you listened, and ask the other person to do the same.

Affirmation Guides and Samples

Calling Tips

Do:
- Know the name of the person you are calling.
- Be acquainted with the ministries of the church.
- Make notes for any follow-up on the assignment sheet.
- Know why you are calling.
- Talk to answering machines by leaving a positive message so the person may be encouraged by the message.

Do Not:
- Debate or defend Christianity, the church, a particular class, or a specific person, but acknowledge the concern of the person.
- Argue with their decision to attend another church, but be thankful that they are attending church somewhere to continue their spiritual well-being).
- Chastise their theology, viewpoint, or decision because each person is entitled to his or her own viewpoints.
- Treat people differently than what you would like to be treated.

Responding to negative calls: "It sounds like you have a legitimate concern." "Can I set up an appointment with a staff member or the pastor so you can talk about it together?" "I understand how you can feel that way."

Calling Samples

Elderly Calls

Step 1 *(Greeting):* "Hi, _____ (name of the person you are calling). This is _____ (your name) from the Lakeland Church. The reason I am calling is to let you know that we care about you. How are you doing today?"

Step 2 *(Dialogue):* Deal with the discussion and/or need in the appropriate way. "Can I pray with you over the phone about anything?" "If there is something that you think that the church can do for you, please do not hesitate to call the church office at 123-456-7890.

Step 3 *(Closing):* Close with a positive comment and thank them for their time on the phone. "Thank you so much for your time. May God bless you."

Step 4 *(Assignment sheet):* Make appropriate detailed notations on the assignment sheet. Return assignment sheet to the team captain at the end of the meeting night for processing by the appropriate staff person.

Unchurched Calls

Step 1 *(Greeting):* "Hi, _____ (name of the person you are calling). This is _____ (your name) from the Lakeland Church. The reason I am calling is to let you know we care about you. How are you doing today?"

Step 2 *(Dialogue):* Deal with the discussion and/or need in the appropriate way. "Do you have a prayer request that we can help you pray about?" If yes, go to step 3. If no, go to step 4.

Step 3 *(Prayer requested):* Write prayer request on the assignment sheet.

Step 4 *(Send information request):* "We're mailing some information to the people in our community to tell them about some of the programs we have for all age groups. Could we send it to you?" If yes, go to step 5. If no, go to step 6.

Step 5   *(Obtain address):* "How would you like for us to address the information?" Write down name with address and what information is to be sent on the assignment sheet.

Step 6   *(Closing):* Close with a positive comment and thank them for their time on the phone. "Thank you so much for your time. May God bless you and remember we do care about you." "If there is something that you think that the church can do for you, please do not hesitate to call the church office at 123-456-7890."

Step 7   *(Assignment sheet):* Make appropriate detailed notations on the assignment sheet. Return assignment sheet to the team captain at the end of the meeting night for processing by the appropriate staff person.

Encouragement Calls

Step 1   *(Greeting):* "Hi, _____ (name of the person you are calling). This is _____ (your name) from the Lakeland Church. The reason I am calling is to let you know we care about you. How are you doing today?"

Step 2   *(Dialogue):* Deal with the discussion and/or need in the appropriate way. Communicate encouragement throughout the discussion. "Is there anything we can pray with you about?"

Step 3   *(Closing):* Close with a positive comment and thanking them for their time on the phone. "Thank you so much for your time. May God bless you and remember that we care." "If there is something that you think that the church can do for you, please do not hesitate to call the church office at 123-456-7890."

Step 4   *(Assignment sheet):* Make appropriate detailed notations on the assignment sheet. Return assignment sheet to the team captain at the end of the meeting night for processing by the appropriate staff person.

Inactive Calls

Step 1 *(Greeting):* "Hi, _____ (name of the person you are calling). This is _____ (your name) from the Lakeland Church. The reason I am calling is our records indicate that you have become inactive by not worshipping with us for several weeks. We hope that you are not ill and that all is going fine."

Step 2 *(Dialogue):* Deal with the discussion in the appropriate way. "I understand what you are talking about." "You mentioned that you are attending another church. Did you join that church?" "Can I pray with you over the phone about anything?"

Step 3 *(Closing):* Close with a positive comment and thanking them for their time on the phone. "Thank you so much for your time. May God bless you." "If there is something that you think that the church can do for you, please do not hesitate to call the church office at 123-456-7890."

Step 4 *(Assignment Sheet):* Make appropriate detailed notations on the assignment sheet. Return assignment sheet to the team captain at the end of the meeting night for processing by the appropriate staff person.

First-Time Visitor Follow-up Calls

Step 1 *(Greeting):* "Hi, _____ (name of the person you are calling). This is _____ (your name) from the Lakeland Church. The reason I am calling is to thank you for visiting with us this past Sunday. Did you have any questions about the information that you received during the worship service?"

Step 2 *(Dialogue):* Deal with the discussion in the appropriate way. "Have you used the ticket for our Wednesday night supper?" "You haven't yet. I invite to come tomorrow because we are having _____ (meal menu). The meal is great, but the fellowship during the meal is even better."

Step 3 *(Closing):* Close with a positive comment and thanking them for their time on the phone. "Thank you so much for your time. May God bless you." "If there is something that you think that the church can do for you, please do not hesitate to call the church office at 123-456-7890."

Step 4 *(Assignment sheet):* Make appropriate detailed notations on the assignment sheet. Return assignment sheet to the team captain at the end of the meeting night for processing by the appropriate staff person.

Prospect Calls

Step 1 *(Greeting):* "Hi, _____ (name of the person you are calling). This is _____ (your name) from the Lakeland Church. The reason I am calling is you indicated an interest in joining the Lakeland Church. I want you to know that we care and I want to try to answer any questions you may have."

Step 2 *(Dialogue):* Deal with the questions as best that you can. If you do not know the answer to a question, let the person know that and you will have someone who has the answers contact them. "I am sorry that I do not know the answer to that question, but I can have one of our ministry people contact you later this week to discuss that question you have." "I understand your concern in that area. At the Lakeland Church we can help you with that issue through one of our ministries (or ministry)." "Can I pray with you over the phone about anything?"

Step 3 *(Closing):* Close with a positive comment and thanking them for their time on the phone. "Thank you so much for your time. May God bless you." "If there is something that you think that the church can do for you, please do not hesitate to call the church office at 123-456-7890."

Step 4 *(Assignment sheet):* Make appropriate detailed notations on the assignment sheet. Return assignment sheet to the team captain at the end of the meeting night for processing by the appropriate staff person.

Hands-On Tips for Work Areas

Do:

- Prepare your heart to serve through prayer.
- Be an encourager.
- Leave area clean and neat for the next person or ministry to use the same space.
- Ask for help if needed.
- Work as a team with the other team members.
- Make notes on the assignment sheets that are clear and concise.

Don't:

- Leave the area unattended.
- Create an unsafe environment by visiting by yourself.
- Speak about something that you are not completely sure about.
- Make commitments that you are not willing to fulfill.

Note: Make sure to follow specific administrative and ministry instructions. Make sure to leave the ministry ready for the next team or person to follow up on.

Hospitality Tips

Do:

- Prepare your heart to serve through prayer.
- Be an encourager.
- Leave area clean and neat for the next person or ministry to use the same space.
- Ask for help if needed.
- Work as a team with the other team members.
- Make notes on the assignment sheets that are clear and concise.
- Maintain constant supervision of any children by at least two adults.
- Ask team members if they need anything.

Don't:

- Leave area unattended.
- Keep needs and problems to yourself.

Note: It is important to keep your area clean and neat. Please handle kids with care. Please put things back in their place before leaving.

Praying Tips

Do:
- Prepare your heart to approach God.
- Gather appropriate stationery and materials.
- Handwrite all affirmation cards.
- Affirm care from the church.
- Personally sign your full name.

Don't:
- Have the wrong perspective on a person's issues.
- Send personal affirmation on postcards for you represent the church and not yourself.

Prayer Card Samples

> *Dear _____,*
> *I prayed for your request tonight. I pray that God will grant it in His own time. Just keep looking up to God.*
>
> > *Sincerely,*
> > *(sign your name)*

> *Dear _____,*
> *I prayed for your request tonight. May God's love be with you, and the request be answered according to God's will.*
>
> > *In Christian love,*
> > *(sign your name)*

Writing Tips

Do:
- Gather appropriate stationery and materials.
- Neatly handwrite and/or print all letters.

- Affirm care from the church.
- Personal sign your name.

Don't:
- Write personal affirmations on postcards because of confidentiality issues.
- Write negative things.

Elderly Sample

> *Dear _____,*
>
> *I just wanted to write to you to let you know how much you are missed here at the Lakeland Church. You are very important to us and we value the heritage and traditions that you share with us. I pray that God will bless you as you go through your day. Please be in prayer for us as we pray for you.*
>
> > *Sincerely,*
> > *(sign your name)*

Special note: Use the above as a sample. Feel free to add your own personal touches. We do not want them to receive the same letter every month.

Encouragement Sample

Each encouragement letter is unique and personal. You may also like to relate a brief testimony of how God helped you through a similar situation or how the person has ministered to you. Keep in mind that you are sending a letter to encourage this person in his or her situation. Keep it as brief as possible and always use a card or letter in a sealed envelope for privacy. No postcards please.

Prospect Sample

First-Time Visitor

> *Dear _____,*
>
> *Thank you for visiting with us at the Lakeland Church. We hope you felt "at home" and that you experienced the presence*

of the Lord. We believe God has commissioned our fellowship to care for the people God sends our way. We want to invite you to visit with us again real soon. If we can help you in any way, please let us know. Our church office number is 123-456-7890. We hope to see you again soon, like this Sunday.

Sincerely,
(sign your name)

Note: Include church information brochure.

Regular Visitor Follow-Up

Dear _____,

Thank you so much for our guest at the Lakeland Church. We just want you to know that we will continue to pray with you as you seek the Lord's will concerning a church home. If we can help you in any way, please let us know. The church office number is 123-456-7890. Again, thank you for your continued interest in our fellowship in Christ's name.

Sincerely,
(sign your name)

Note: Include church information brochure.

Sympathy Sample

Dear _____,

We at the Lakeland Church express to you our deepest sympathy upon the recent loss of your loved one. We are praying for you and your family. If we can help you in any way, please feel free to call our church at 123-456-7890. May God bless you, and may the Holy Spirit comfort you at this time.

In Christ's love,
(sign your name)

Visiting Tips

Do:

- Gather appropriate tracts and materials.
- Get directions from a map or map program.
- Go two by two.
- Be gender conscience (two men should not visit a female).
- Remember that the visit is to be no more than thirty minutes for the formal visits and no more than five minutes with visitors.
- Pray for the person you are going to visit prior to making the visit.
- Rehearse your opening lines before approaching the home.

Don't:

- Go into the house unless invited in by the tenant(s).
- Debate or defend Christianity, the church, a particular class, or a specific person, but acknowledge the concern of the person.
- Argue with their decision to attend another church, but be thankful that they are attending church somewhere to continue their spiritual well-being).
- Chastise their theology, viewpoint, or decision because each person is entitled to his or her own viewpoints.
- Treat people differently from what you would like to be treated.
- Pray, unless given permission by the person(s) you are visiting.

The Visit

If Home:

Step 1 *(Greeting):* "Hi, I am _____ (your name) and this is _____. We are from the Lakeland Church. We are here to _____ (reason for visit)."

> **First-Time Visitor Reason**: "We are here to thank you for visiting with us this past Sunday. We also want to invite you to come back to worship with us real soon."

Prospect Reason: "We are here to thank you for inquiring about _____ (church membership or relationship with Christ)."

Inactive Reason: "We are here because our records show that you have not been to _____ Church to worship in several weeks. We want to let you know that we miss you."

Un-churched Reason: "We are friends of _____ (person requesting the visit) and we want to invite you to attend one of our Sunday worship services."

Step 2 *(Dialogue):* Deal with the discussion in the appropriate way. Verbally affirm care and discern needs. "Can we pray with you? Is there anything specific you would like to pray about?"

Step 3 *(Closing):* Close with a positive comment and thanking them for their time on the phone. "Thank you so much for your time. May God bless you."

Step 4 *(Assignment sheet):* Make appropriate detailed notations on the assignment sheet. Return assignment sheet to the team captain at the end of the meeting night for processing by the appropriate staff person.

If Not Home:

Leave church information with a handwritten postcard. Upon return to the church, please make appropriate detailed notations on assignment sheet and return assignment sheet to the team captain.

Confidentiality

Why Is Confidentiality Important?

- Protect members' privacy.
- Stops embarrassing situations from being disclosed.
- Prevents improper information dissemination.
- Personal and family security.
- Avoids prejudice or differential treatment.

- Encourages people to come to church.

What Are the Confidentiality Limits?
- When it could seriously hamper helping the individual.
- When there are suicide threats or physical abuse concerns.
- When you think a law is being violated.

How Should Dilemmas Be Addressed?
- Do not share with anyone else.
- Contact the team captain. If the team captain is not present, then contact the pastor.

Improvements

As we care, we will discover ways to be more efficient, effective, and affirming through our care. If you see, hear, or experience something as you conduct this ministry that is detrimental to our caring ministry, take the necessary steps to correct the issue.

If you have a way that we can improve our caring ministry, please write it down and give it to the team captain. The team captain will discuss your improvement with the Lay Advisory Committee.

Remember that we can care only as much as you are willing to. Let us glorify God by using the love, grace, and mercy that God has blessed us with as we care for those we come in contact with.

Thank you for using those gifts. Thank you for taking up the mantle of responsibility of caring. Thank God for you pursuing God's will in your life through this caring ministry!

Weekly Team Meeting Agenda

6:30 p.m.: Assemble in the Worship Center

6:30–6:35 p.m.:
Welcome
Team prayer
Team assignments

6:35–8:10 p.m.: Caring Ministry

8:10–8:15 p.m.: Assemble in the Worship Center

8:10–8:25 p.m.: Team celebration (directed interviews conducted as visiting subteams come in)

8:25–8:30 p.m.: Dismissed

Appendix H

Listening Skills Forms

These forms were used during the listening skills portion of the training phase. They aid in conducting the listening skills training. Each volunteer shares the information on both forms. See the training slides in appendix I for the use of these forms.

Form A

My name is _____.

My immediate family includes _____

_____

_____.

My job in the local church is _____

_____

_____.

My occupation is _____.

Form B

What I am proud about in my church is_____

_____

_____ .

When I call on strangers, I feel _____

_____

_____ .

The thing I like most about myself is_____

_____

_____ .

I am happiest when_____

_____

_____ .

Appendix I
Training Sessions

These slides were used during the training sessions. They can be modified to pertain to your particular style of training. The content can be changed to accommodate any additional training needs that you identify.

Training Session 1

Slide 1

Caring Ministry

Becoming a Caregiver Today!

Session One

Note: Clip art and/or pictures are useful here.

Slide 2

Training Agenda

- Welcome.
- Team Member Notebook distribution.
- What is the Caring Ministry?
- Five Avenues of Contact.
- Team Meeting Agenda.
- Principles of Calling and Visiting.
- Purpose of the Caring Ministry.
- Relationship Building.

- Questions.

Slide 3

What Is The Caring Ministry?

- Is not another program about someone's personality, a ministry substitute or alternative, or quick fix.
- Is an ongoing ministry that mobilizes church members, supports current ministries, and improves our church's health.
- Body of Christ: 1 Corinthians 12:12 and 26 = "For as the body is one and has many members, but all the members of that one body, being many, are one body, so also is Christ. And if one member suffers, all the members suffer with it; or if one member is honored, all the members rejoice with it."

Slide 4

Avenues of Contact

- In-reach: Needs with members (inactives, encouragement).
- Out-reach: Encourage visitors to return to worship and ministry events and regular visitors to become church members.
- Hands-On: Putting faith into action.
- Prayer: Holy grease for the work to be done through this caring ministry.

Slide 5

Team Meeting Agenda

- 6:30 p.m.: Assemble in the Worship Center.
- 6:30–6:35 p.m.
  - Welcome.
  - Team prayer.
  - Team assignments.

- 6:35–8:10 p.m.: Caring is being conducted.
- 8:10–8:15 p.m.: Assemble in the Worship Center.
- 8:15–8:30 p.m.: Team celebration.

Slide 6

Calling Principles

- Have to **call.**
- Don't have to be **pushy.**
- Don't **embarrass** the recipient.
- Remember the person's **name.**
- Remember this improves our **church health.**

This is critical since this may be the first contact from the church that an inactive member has had for months or years. This helps get the relationship building off on a good note.

Slide 7

Visiting Principles

- Have to **go.**
- Don't have to be **pushy.**
- Don't **embarrass** the recipient.
- Biblical **pairs.**
- Remember the person's **name.**
- Remember this improves our **church health.**

The visits (formal and informal) are critical to continued relationship building. They are the practical means by which we demonstrate God's love for them.

Slide 8

Purpose of the Caring Ministry

- Relationship Building:
  This will only occur if you are genuine in seeing people grow in their Christian walk.
- Principle of putting people first:
  To win their trust, they must come first in word and deed. Show genuine interest in their interests, stories, and lives.
- Look to build relationships: Not just on your Caring Ministry nights but in daily living through our chance contacts.

Slide 9

Questions

Training Session 2

Slide 1

Caring Ministry

Becoming a Caregiver Today!

Session 1

Note: Clip art and/or pictures are useful here.

Slide 2

Training Agenda

- Welcome.
- Purpose.

- Viewpoints of Active and Inactive Members.
- Team Member Familiarization.
- Relationship Building.
- Listening Skills Development.
- Role-Playing.
- Confidentiality.
- Questions.

Slide 3

Purpose of the Caring Ministry

- Relationship Building:
    This will only occur if you are genuine
    in seeing people grow in their Christian walk.
- Principle of putting people first:
    To win their trust, they must come first in word and deed.
    Show genuine interest in their interests, stories, and lives.
- Look to build relationships: Not just on your Caring Ministry nights but in daily living through our chance contacts.

Slide 4

Member Familiarization

What do you think of inactive members?

Slide 5

Member Familiarization

Active Members think Inactive Members are:
- Dropouts
- Delinquents
- Do-Nothings
- Inactive

- Lazy
- Backsliders
- Sinners
- Complainers
- Excuse makers

Slide 6

Member Familiarization

When dealing with Inactive Members, how do you feel?

Slide 7

Member Familiarization

When dealing with Inactive Members, Active Members feel:

- Frustrated
- Fearful
- Anxious
- Worried
- Hostile
- Suspicious
- Full of pity
- Sympathetic
- Puzzled
- Embarrassed

Slide 8

Member Familiarization

What do Inactive Members think of Active Members?

Slide 9

Member Familiarization

Inactive Members think Active Members are:

- Hypocrites
- Do-Gooders
- Nosy
- Fussy
- Nitpickers
- Bosses
- The *In* Group
- Judges
- High and Mighty
- Meddlers

Slide 10

Member Familiarization

When dealing with Active Members, Inactive Members feel:

- Condemned
- Forgotten
- Left Out
- Lonely
- Rejected
- Abandoned
- Angry
- Suspicious
- Like Failures
- Apathetic
- Like They Do Not Care

Slide 11

Member Familiarization

Team Member Introductions (ten minutes)

Note: Team members fill out form A. The team members pair up and introduce themselves to each other. After ten minutes, the team members introduce their partner to the rest of the team.

Slide 12

Member Familiarization

Member Perceptions (two minutes each)

Note: Team members fill out form B. Each team member informs the rest of the team what their answers to the questions are.

Slide 13

Listening Skills

Pay attention:
- Comfortable tone
- Body language
- Respect

Withhold judgment:
- Open mind
- Hold your criticism
- Avoid arguing

Reflect:
- Paraphrase key points
- Don't assume your understanding

Clarify:
- Ask questions about any unclear issue
- Invite reflection and thoughtful response
- Positive use of questions
- Connect to the speaker's feelings

Summarize:
- Restate key themes
- Clear on mutual responsibilities and follow-up

Slide 14

Practice Conversations

Role-Playing:
- Visitor
- Inactive Member
- Observer

Note: Divide the team into groups of three people. Each team member will serve in each of the above capacities. Use the role-playing scenarios to facilitate different types of encounters.

Slide 15

Practice Conversations

Critique:
- All are learning
- Listen to the Speaker
- Avoid arguing

Note: Each group of three will conduct the role-playing. After each scenario is played out (the training facilitator will stop the role-playing scenario when appropriate), the team member serving as the observer will tell the entire team what was observed that was good and what could have been done differently. After the observer is finished, then the training facilitator will ask for the next scenario to be conducted.

Slide 16

Practice Conversations

Differences of Real Visit Compared to Role-Playing:
- Go out in two-person subteams
- Appointment is made with Inactive Members
- Only "cold calls" are with first-time visitors.

Slide 17

Confidentiality

Why is it important?
- Protects members' privacy.
- Stops embarrassing situations from being disclosed.
- Prevents improper information dissemination.
- Personal and family security.
- Avoids prejudice or differential treatment.
- Encourages people to come to church.

What are the limits to it?
- When it could seriously hamper helping the individual.
- When there are suicide threats or physical abuse.
- When you think a law is being violated.

How should confidentiality dilemmas be addressed?
- Do not share with anyone else.
- Contact the team captain or the pastor.

Slide 18

Questions

Appendix J

Role-Playing Scenarios

These scenarios were used during the role-playing portion of the second training session. As discussed in the changes, this portion would be expanded with more possible scenarios. These scenarios can be adapted to pertain to your congregation and/or culture.

The trainer arbitrarily assigns the situations to each volunteer to act out in a role-playing scenario with another volunteer. All volunteers observe what occurs. At the trainer's discretion, the trained can stop the role-playing and conduct a review of what the volunteers have learned. This allows all volunteers to learn from each other.

Situation 1: You are a married middle-aged person. You have stopped coming to church because you are frustrated that your family does not come to church with you. This causes you to be embarrassed by seeing other families coming to church together. Your spouse is a heavy drinker. Children no longer live in the home. You are friendly to other church members and continue to provide food for the hospitality committee. However you will not come back to church until your family comes with you.

Situation 2: You are a senior citizen and have been a member of the church for over sixty years. About thirty years ago, you stopped active participation in the church because you were embarrassed by a layperson during a church committee meeting. You have vowed never to come back to church because no one cares about you. You are not open to active participation at all, but you want your name left on the rolls so there is a pastor who will have to do your funeral when you die.

Situation 3: You are a young person whose spouse died two years ago from cancer. You blame God for the spouse's death. You are grateful for the care that the church showed following the death and funeral. You admire the pastor who conducted the funeral service. You struggle with God being a loving God because God allowed the cancer that took your spouse. This struggle has caused you to stop coming to a place that worships the One that took the love of your life from you. For the last year, no one from the church has contacted you.

Situation 4: You stopped coming after the pastor preached a sermon about you. Everyone knows that the person in the sermon was you. That pastor is such a hypocrite to talk about love and compassion from the pulpit, only to turn around and tell the church about a situation in your life that was supposed to be confidential. You believe all pastors are the same. You have not thought about your name on the roll, but you refuse to respond to any of the church's letters.

Situation 5: You have gotten angry with the church members who act *oh so holy* on Sunday and like demons the rest of the week. You are so tired of sitting in church with these hypocrites that it makes you sick. The church is filled with nothing but do-gooders who do good for themselves and no one else. How can the preacher put up with these hypocrites? How can God continue to let these people run the church? You want to remain on the church rolls because everyone belongs to a church, even though they do not go.

Situation 6: You were active until you changed jobs. You now work locally but have to work every weekend. You would like to get back to church, but right now there is no chance of that occurring. You send a tithe check into the church after each pay period. You pray over the prayer list each week. You are keeping up with the pastor's Read the Bible in a Year challenge. You would be at the church every time the doors open if it were not for this well paying job.

Situation 7: You grew up in the church. You were active in the youth group. Then you went to college and joined the military. When you left the military, you came back to your hometown. You attended the old church again. Then you got married and had children. You have not been in the church in over forty years. As a senior citizen, you are concerned about where you will be for eternity, but you really do not want to answer questions about your lack of church attendance for the last forty years.

Situation 8: You were active in the youth group for several years. You went off to college. While in college, you became a practicing homosexual. You do not like the stance of the UMC on homosexuals. However you want your name left on the church rolls so your parents do not get upset with you. You will never come back to the church because you are not comfortable around those closed-minded people.

Situation 9: You have been a church member for several years. You attended about once a month. You make sure you attend church on Easter and around Christmas with your family. You got into drugs. Now you have to work extra hours to make enough money to support your drug habit. This means that your church attendance has decreased to just Easter and Christmas … sometimes. You want help but are not sure whom to turn to. However you conceal your drug habit from your family and friends and hope that no one will know.

Situation 10: You have gotten bored with church. The pastor is not a good preacher. You do not get anything out of the sermons, prayers, or hymns. The music is terrible because it is all those old hymns that do not relate to you. You know that you should go because it is the right thing to do, but you are not motivated to go. You want excitement and variety, but that will never happen at church. You want your name on the rolls so you will get into heaven. You throw all church correspondence away because you are not going to respond to it anyway. You might go back to church if it could be like a rock concert.

Situation 11: You are married and a senior citizen. Your days are filled with being at the nursing home to tend to your spouse. Every day you are at the nursing home at 8 a.m. and do not leave until after 7 p.m. This is how you demonstrate love for your spouse. You feel it is what you need to be doing right now. This means that your active church attendance has declined to nothing.

Situation 12: You found out that you caused someone to leave the church because of an action that you did to him or her. You are afraid that you will cause others to leave the church as well. You think that it is better if you leave so others can stay. You feel like an embarrassment to God for what has occurred. You cannot bring yourself to go back to the church, not even for special events. You think that maybe one day you will be able to go back so you want your name left on the church rolls. One day you may go back, but not anytime soon.

Appendix K

Introductory Letter

Note: This form letter was placed on church letterhead with the pastor's signature.

We have begun a new caring ministry, which is designed to reach all of our church members. We would like one of our visitation groups to visit you in the near future to reconnect with you as one of our church members. We are not asking you for money or coercing you into coming back into active church participation. It is simply our way of rebuilding a relationship with you.

I have enclosed a self-addressed, stamped response card for you to indicate if you are open to this visit. If you agree or not, please send the card back to indicate your desire. If you agree, then one of our visitation groups will contact you to schedule a visit. Please send this card back to us by _____.

Our prayer is that we are able to reestablish a relationship with you so that we both can prosper as God's children. You are needed and wanted here! We would like to grow in our faith together with you.

We look forward to reconnecting with you so that we can serve God together in making our communities a better place to live, work, and play. May God richly bless you today and forevermore!

Faithfully,

_____

Senior Pastor

Appendix L
Response Card

Note: This response card accompanies the introductory letter. This card is a self-addressed and stamped postcard. It requires the inactive member to check their response, sign it, and mail it back to the church.

Response Card

Place an X indicating your choice:

_____ I am open to a visit by a visitation group. I understand that I will receive a call to coordinate this visit.

_____ I do not want a visit by a visitation group.

_____ I would like to meet with the pastor.

_____ I have joined another church: (name and address of church)

_____

_____

_____

_____ I wish to withdraw my membership.

Signed: _____

Appendix M
Visitation Report Forms

These report forms provide feedback from the volunteers on their perceptions about the visits or contacts.

The formal visit report form is used for the first (formal) visit with the inactive members. This form is returned to the team captain upon return to conclude the caring ministry night. This form helps in conducting the post-visit debriefing.

Formal Visit Report Form

Note: The formal visit report form is used when a formal visit is conducted. This form provides information and perceptions of the visiting group about the visit. This form is reproduced and attached to the assignment sheet for each visiting subteam. If possible, a map highlighting the best route should be provided to aid in finding the home for the visit.

The items needed for the report form are:
- Name of person being visited;
- Address of person to be visited;
- Telephone number of person to be visited;
- Team name assigned to;
- Was visit well received? Comment required;
- Did he/she give a reason for becoming inactive? If yes, please provide the reason;
- Were ways to improve our church ministries provided by the person being visited? If yes, provide the way;
- Was a pastor visit requested? and
- Was a relationship established? Provide perceptions about the visit.

Informal Visit Report Form

Note: The informal visit report form is used each week to determine if informal contacts occurred and/or the perception of the visiting group about the informal visit.

The items needed for the report form are:
- Name of person being visited;
- Address of person to be visited;
- Telephone number of person to be visited;
- Team name assigned to;
- Was visit well received? Comment required;
- Did he/she give a reason for becoming inactive? If yes, please provide the reason;
- Were ways to improve our church ministries provided by the person being visited? If yes, provide the way;
- Was a pastor visit requested?
- Was a relationship developed and/or improved? Provide perceptions about the contact; and
- Other details or perceptions about the contact.

About the Author

Dr. Richard Wright is a parish pastor in the South Georgia Annual Conference of the United Methodist Church. He has served in small, rural churches up to large, metropolitan churches. He earned a master of divinity degree from Candler School of Theology at Emory University in Atlanta, Georgia. He earned a doctor of ministry degree in evangelism and missions from Austin Presbyterian Theological Seminary in Austin, Texas. His passion is lay empowerment and evangelism. His desire is to see the body of Christ growing and maturing because its members are sharing God's love with the world.

Prior to becoming a pastor, Richard served as an Airborne Ranger infantryman in the US Army's rapid deployment units where in combat he earned a Bronze Star and the Combat Infantryman's Badge. After his military service and while working for an international logistics corporation, he attended Discover God's Call where he discovered his spiritual gifts while learning that God was guiding him toward ordained ministry. Since then, his endeavors have been to preach and teach about how we can experience the saving power of God through Jesus Christ.

Richard and his wife, Ruth, currently reside in Hinesville, Georgia, where he is the senior pastor of Hinesville First United Methodist Church.